BUILDING DANCES

A GUIDE TO PUTTING MOVEMENTS TOGETHER

Susan McGreevy-Nichols
Roger Williams Middle School
Providence, Rhode Island

Helene Scheff
Dance Alliance/Chance to Dance
Providence, Rhode Island

Human Kinetics

Library of Congress Cataloging-in-Publication Data

McGreevy-Nichols, Susan, 1952-
    Building dances : a guide to putting movements together / Susan McGreevy-Nichols, Helene Scheff.
        p.   cm.
    ISBN 0-87322-573-2 (paper)
    1. Dance for children--Study and teaching (Elementary)   2. Dance--Study and teaching (Secondary)   3. Choreography--Study and teaching (Elementary)   4. Choreography--Study and teaching (Secondary)
    5. Movement education.   I. Scheff, Helene, 1939-   .   II. Title.
    GV1799.M3   1995
    792.2'083--dc20   95-8141
                                                                             CIP

ISBN: 0-87322-573-2

Acquisitions and Developmental Editor: Judy Patterson Wright, PhD, **Assistant Editors:** Karen Bojda and John Wentworth, **Copyeditor:** Frances Purifoy, **Proofreader:** Karen Bojda, **Typesetter and Layout Artist:** Kathy Boudreau-Fuoss, **Text Designer:** Judy Henderson, **Cover Designer:** Jack Davis, **Illustrator:** Dick Flood, **Diagrams:** Craig Ronto, **Printer:** United Graphics

Human Kinetics books are available at special discounts for bulk purchase. Special editions or book excerpts can also be created to specification. For details, contact the Special Sales Manager at Human Kinetics.

Printed in the United States of America   10 9 8 7 6 5 4 3 2 1

Human Kinetics
P.O. Box 5076, Champaign, IL 61825-5076
1-800-747-4457

Canada: Human Kinetics, Box 24040, Windsor, ON N8Y 4Y9
1-800-465-7301 (in Canada only)

Europe: Human Kinetics, P.O. Box IW14, Leeds LS16 6TR, United Kingdom
(44) 1132 781708

Australia: Human Kinetics, 2 Ingrid Street, Clapham 5062
South Australia, (08) 371 3755

New Zealand: Human Kinetics, P.O. Box 105-231, Auckland 1
(09) 523 3462

Contents

Preface

Think of *Building Dances* as your architect's manual . . . a novice's guide to choreography. All the necessary tools and building materials are in it. All you need to add to the nine dance construction models are the kids. Use their input and ideas as architectural details, the fancy scrollwork, the impressive facade. Don't be afraid to experiment. If all the foundation materials are in place, the building will not fall, and you can be successful. There is no wrong way! Nothing is as rewarding as seeing students at any level bring a concept through the creative process under your guidance. When you make a game or puzzle of the dance construction process, you and your students benefit from a creative experience that challenges critical thinking skills and the artistic impulse.

Dance is defined by the second edition of the Random House Dictionary as "to move one's feet or body, or both, rhythmically in a pattern of steps, especially to the accompaniment of music." In simpler terms, dance is movement created and executed to satisfy a need. It can be stylized, done to music or not, tell a story or not, create images, use space, define moods, create and channel energy. The nine dance construction models in this book enable the dance movements to take on a shape, create a scene, communicate a story, foster an idea, or interpret a piece of music. These movements, which are created through the use of dance construction models, can use the entire body or various body parts in isolation or together. They can range from very basic moves, such as walking, sitting, arm waving, and so on, to more complicated dance moves, such as leaps and turns. A dance, the result of a lesson using a dance construction model, can move simply in one direction or use a very intricate floor pattern.

In both private and public education, dance is an under-served discipline. It constantly gets caught between the cracks. Where does it belong in the established subject areas? Ideally, it should be treated as a separate entity taught by certified dance educators or dance specialists. In actuality, a recent national survey showed that the responsibility of teaching dance falls to physical educators, theater or English teachers, music educators, and classroom teachers, as well as to dance educators.

The dance construction models in this book were developed to satisfy the needs expressed by five constituencies: physical education teachers, drama teachers and coaches, classroom teachers, music teachers, and dance teachers. As a by-product of these needs, the authors saw an even wider range of people who could use these models in many ways. These include recreation and community center personnel who desire to have students experience the joy of moving in a variety of ways and of creating their own dances. Many of these dance construction models have been presented at conferences to several of the constituencies mentioned above with great success. In addition, these models have been tested on children from grades K-12, all of whom have proven to be receptive participants. Children love to perform and, given the opportunity, will amaze you with their ability. By creating a dance in each of your classes, you will have enough material to put on a dance performance that will charm students, teachers, and parents alike. Read on to see how you can use this book to challenge your students!

Acknowledgments

The authors would like to thank the following: Joseph Maguire, principal at Roger Williams Middle School, Providence, RI, for his support and belief that dance as a separate endeavor should be part of *every* child's school day; the students at Roger Williams Middle School for being the willing subjects of experimenting with new creative ideas and programs over the past 20 years; the children of South County Players Children's Theater, RI; the students at Kingstown Dance Center, North Kingstown, RI; Chris Wilde and Patricia Grant Cohen for proofreading; Marty Sprague; Daniel Scheff; Kendra Jackson; Rae Pica for encouraging this book; attendees of AAHPERD, RIAHPERD, and NHAHPERD conferences; and finally, Schlep and Schlock.

Blueprints for Building a Dance— How to Use This Book

If you've never done it before, the thought of creating your own dance from scratch can be very intimidating. But, just like building a house, "building a dance" (as choreography has been called) can be manageable and even a fun process when you have the proper tools, some basic skills, and a plan. This book is designed to serve as a blueprint to guide you and your students through the process of building a dance.

Special Features

This book is unique because it becomes a hands-on tool that invites and cultivates variety and creativity within given structures. Each section of the book is summarized for easy reference. A glossary is included that explains many special dance terms in everyday language. Parts of a lesson, lesson plans, and student outcomes/student assessment forms are included. The unique Deal-a-Dance card deck (with 224 movement examples) can be used as a teacher's guide or an interactive classroom tool to stimulate your students' imaginations as they try to build dances.

In Part I, "Laying a Foundation," you will be introduced to the relationship between creativity and choreography, how to facilitate creativity, and the three parts of dance. In Part II, "Identifying Building Supplies," you will become acquainted with movement skills and elements, ethnic and cultural influences, historical and social perspectives, and ways of organizing music to facilitate choreography. All these materials and tools will assist the choreographic process.

Part III, "Constructing the Frame and Roof," familiarizes you with structure of dances and choreographic forms, how story lines and characterizations can be the basis for some dances, and how the use of sound and props can enhance choreography. Part IV, "Adding the Architectural Details," explains and clarifies the use of accenting, gestures, stylizing, and expressive qualities in the choreographic process. Part V, "Putting It All Together," leads you through the seven steps to building a dance, from the birth of an idea through the performance.

Part VI, "Inspecting Your Creation," gives you yet another set of blueprints; these are for evaluation and assessment. Finally, Part VII, "Building Dances From Sample Blueprints," supplies nine fun ways of implementing choreography through dance construction models. Each one is a learning experience using basic skills and concepts. Each one is a fun experience designed to be nonthreatening to both teacher and student. Each one encourages some aspect of the creative process. Each one addresses specific developmental skills. Each one puts the teacher in the role of facilitator, not necessarily demonstrator. Each one has sections labeled activity/procedure, example activity, grade-appropriate adaptations, and learner outcomes/student assessment. These sections guide the facilitator to maximize the learning experience. Communicating with the students is a constant source of inspiration. Their willingness to cooperate and bring their thoughts and ideas to the class make every day a rewarding, exciting, and fulfilling experience.

In Part VII, any of the dance construction models can be used within a single lesson, as a dance unit, as a full semester, or as a year-long program. They can also be used in building a dance curriculum. Each dance construction model is briefly described below.

- *Deal-a-Dance* has as its structural support a series of 112 playing cards that are divided into four categories (see enclosed cards). These categories are dance techniques, elements that change movements, sports and game movements, and creative movement suggestions. The information on both the front and the back of these playing cards (224 movement examples) provides the raw material you need in working with all the construction models. They describe the basic movement skills and elements needed to facilitate choreography. The versatility of the cards makes every dance class an adventure.

- *Picture Dance* uses pictures as a source of positions and movements for creating dances.

- *Words, Sentences, and Paragraphs* bridge the gap between language and movement, and provide opportunities for team teaching with classroom teachers.
- *Story Dance* invites a three-dimensional interpretation of literature and hones storytelling skills.
- *Write What I See* develops observation and writing skills.
- *Machine Dance* fosters cooperative learning through the creation of imaginary, visual robotics. It also can introduce the use of sounds to enhance the creative process.
- *Prop Dance* uses articles of clothing and small hand-held items to play on preconceived notions and attitudes in order to help students get started and be more comfortable with moving in creative ways.
- *Decode-a-Dance* introduces aesthetic criticism as a means of understanding dance as an art form.
- *Create-a-Culture* adds a new twist to multicultural education and can play a significant role in the understanding of what makes up a culture.

Threefold Purpose

The primary focus of this book is to demystify the process of choreography and to help you find a comfort zone that will enable you to teach the process within a dance unit. Our approach puts the educator in the role of facilitator, rather than demonstrator—one who is responsible for making something take place. Using the dance construction models detailed in this book, the teacher explains the material, teaches the necessary skills, goes over the procedure, directs the action, analyzes the results, and assesses the outcomes; while the students do the creative work.

Secondly, this book is a reference tool that introduces the basics of choreography through a series of developmentally appropriate dance construction models; it is applicable to any grade K-12 situation. Our aim was to use the material in this book to "dangle a carrot in front of a donkey's nose" . . . inspiring users to want to learn more. We hope you will become excited about choreography and dance and therefore will want to bring professionals into your facility to choreograph and interact with your students.

Thirdly, this book can help satisfy many of the dance content standards as part of the National Standards for Art Education. With the passage of the Goals 2000: Educate America Act, the arts are written into federal law and acknowledged as a core subject. Title II of the act addresses the issue of education standards. In 1992, the Consortium of National Arts Education Associations developed the National Education Standards for the Arts as a guide to help teachers identify children's expected knowledge and competence in the arts. The resulting book, *National Standards for the Arts Education: What Every Young American Should Know and Be Able to Do in the Arts*, is available for purchase through the Music Educators National Conference by calling 1-800-828-0229. This book not only addresses the standards for dance but also for music, theater, and the visual arts. The national standards for dance consist of the following seven content standards:

1. Identifying and demonstrating movement elements and skills in performing dance
2. Understanding choreographic principles, processes, and structures
3. Understanding dance as a way to create and communicate meaning
4. Applying and demonstrating critical and creative thinking skills in dance
5. Demonstrating and understanding dance in various cultures and historical periods
6. Making connections between dance and healthful living
7. Making connections between dance and other disciplines

Under each content standard there are a number of achievement standards which specify the understanding levels of achievement that students are expected to attain at the completion of grades 4, 8, and 12. The resulting framework can act as a guide when designing a comprehensive dance program.

You can use *Building Dances* to satisfy the various content standards. For example, Deal-a-Dance (found in Part VII and in the attached card deck) can be used (a) in grades K-4 to teach children various locomotor and nonlocomotor movements and dance elements, (b) in grades 5-8 to help students combine movements to create simple dances and to use dance as a way to communicate meaning, or (c) in grades 9-12 to help students understand and apply various choreographic principles, as they are engaged in the creative process. Students can discuss what they like about the dances and how they can change them.

Other examples include using Create-a-Culture (in Part VII) to foster discussion among junior high students about their own cultures as they create an expression of their own invented culture. Or, you might select the Story Dance (in Part VII) to help students use dance to create meaningful communication as well as make connections to drama, art, and writing when they create an original children's story with costumes, scenery, advertisements, program booklets, and reviews. The students could perform their stories for a neighborhood elementary school. Use the performance checklist (found in Part VI) to help evaluate the piece.

Whether you're a physical education teacher, drama teacher or coach, music teacher, dance teacher, classroom teacher, or recreation specialist, this book is for you. Use it to help students experience both the joy of moving in a variety of ways and the satisfaction of creating their own dances.

PART I

Laying a Foundation–
Specs and Codes

This section answers the following questions:

- What makes a dance?
- What is choreography?
- How is creativity facilitated?
- How can day-to-day dance classes be implemented?
- How can these classes be built using specific learner outcomes?
- How can the students be assessed on the basis of these outcomes?

The Relationship
Between Creativity and Choreography

Choreography is the art of building dances, and the choreographer is the architect. Creativity figures strongly in this building process, for the more creative, inventive, and flexible the choreographer, the more versatile the dance. Once you become comfortable building simple dances, with creativity you can make them more complex. A sense of adventure and imagination makes the sky the limit.

By learning to organize your thoughts and materials, you can begin the creative process. Small starts and steps can lead to wonderful choreography. Also remember that choreography evolves and changes, and there is no right or wrong. Guiding students through the building of a dance allows you to be part of the creative process, making the experience a truly collaborative effort between teacher and students.

How to Facilitate Creativity

Creativity doesn't mean that thoughts and gestures are pulled from the air in an unorganized manner. To foster productive creativity, you should set guidelines using a problem-solving format. Two methods that facilitate creativity are the use of imagery and brainstorming.

Imagery can be invaluable in helping you envision what a movement should look like. The following are sample questions to stimulate imagery and creativity.

- How does a snowflake look as it falls to the ground?
- How do tree branches look on a mild, breezy day? In a hurricane (see Figure 1.1)?
- What do you see when you think of a school yard full of children?

Brainstorming is a problem-solving method. Gathering information through unrestricted and spontaneous discussion stimulates creative thinking and aids in developing new ideas or ways of solving a choreographic problem. Use the following steps to facilitate creativity:

Step	Example
1. Determine problem	Create a dance showing conflict.

Figure 1.1   Some trees are calm and flowing. Others move more sharply in response to the elements.

2. Brainstorm   Discuss the following: What constitutes a conflict? What does your body feel like during conflict? What image pops into your mind when you think of conflict? What gestures would you use during a confrontation? What facial expressions denote a conflict? Would the movements be smooth or sharp, fast or slow, small or large?

3. Improvise/   To improvise is to compose without prepara-
   explore   tion or forethought or on the spot, without
   movement   being directed. The dancers move in ways that
   possibilities   they believe best tell their feelings or story.
                     Improvisation can also result from listening to the music and reacting from within. Use improvisation to create three movements, one that moves from place to place, a second frozen in place (pose), and a third that must turn. All moves must convey conflict.

4. Develop   Link the three movements and repeat the
   choreography   series three times in a row.

Use these steps with any subject matter or abstract idea.

Three Parts of a Lesson

As with any physical education class, a dance class has three sections: warm-up, activity, and cooldown. The general information that follows serves as a support structure for lesson planning.

Warm-Up

Although as educators and adults we know the value and necessity of a proper warm-up before any physical activity, we must stress the importance of a careful warm-up to our students. Children are taught that warming up the muscles before a football, baseball, or soccer game, or stretching before running or jogging is necessary and beneficial, and because dance is also a physical activity, dance educators should emphasize that warming up is equally important before dancing.

Because children tend to be impressed by visuals and imagery, you can relate the following comparisons to "cold" muscles:

Example 1: Ask the students if they have ever handled "Silly Putty." How difficult is it to pull the putty when it is cold, and what happens when you try to stretch it quickly? you might ask. (It snaps in two.) Then ask them what happens after you warm the putty in your hand for several minutes. (You suddenly find that it is pliable and offers little resistance to stretching.) Explain that human muscle is like "Silly Putty" and that taking the time to warm the muscles before exercising makes using them easier and more efficient.

Example 2: Tap dancers (hoofers) once thought they didn't have to warm up. After all, they really didn't stretch or exert their muscles. The late Sammy Davis, Jr., once said that if he had known of the need for proper warm-up and had done so regularly, he probably wouldn't have needed hip replacement surgery.

Students should know what is needed for a complete warm-up. The following foundation-building components should be included, in the order listed:

1. Lubricate each joint, exploring full range of motion and using gentle movements.
2. Use aerobic movements—repetitive movements bringing blood flow to large muscle groups. Only when there is adequate blood flow to the muscles can you begin to stretch.
3. Stretch large muscle groups.

4. Use crunches and curl downs for strength. (These could also be done at the beginning of cooldown instead of the end of warm-up.)

Activity

Whichever activity is selected as the main focus of your lesson, use the following general progression:

1. Introduce a movement skill.
2. Introduce a movement element.
3. Create a movement pattern using skills and elements.
4. Have students explore use of movement skills and elements using problem-solving techniques.

Cooldown

Use the cooldown segment of your lesson to accomplish the following:

1. After strenuous activity the muscles and cardiovascular system need to return to normal. Students should continue a slow activity until their breathing and heart rate are normal.
2. Students need a calming conclusion to the physical activity before returning to their academic activities.
3. During this time, students and teachers can reflect on the lesson of the day and on what has been learned.

Safety Tips

Stress the following safety practices at every level during all warm-up and dance activities.

1. When doing knee bends (pliés), keep knees over the toes.
2. When doing any kind of jump, start from bent knees (plié) and land with bent knees (in plié).
3. Align the spine properly in every exercise. Avoid a hyper-extended back or a forward-thrust pelvis.
4. Always make sure there is adequate blood flow to the muscles before stretching.
5. Make sure shoulders are relaxed and pulled down. Avoid hunching by shortening the neck.

6. If during any movement throughout the lesson you feel pain, stop immediately.

7. Take time to cool down by continuing to walk. (Students' heart rates return to normal at different times. Students should be encouraged to take whatever time they need to cool down adequately and to be aware and in charge of their own bodies.)

Three Sample Lesson Plans

Grades K-3

WARM-UP

This teacher-facilitated warm-up is designed to give children the necessary tools to create their own developmentally correct warm-ups for future use. Before beginning a warm-up, lay down the ground rules: Make no sharp movements of the neck, always make the knees face the same direction as the toes, and make movements gentle.

1. The lubrication portion of the warm-up includes an inventory of the joints and muscles and an exploration of how they can be moved. Starting with the top of the body, ask the students how many ways they can move

   - their heads and necks;
   - their shoulders;
   - their arms, elbows, and wrists;
   - their torso;
   - their hips and legs; and
   - their knees, ankles, and feet.

   (This exploration can also be done from bottom to top.)

2. The aerobic portion of a warm-up includes

   - alternate jogging in place and freezing,
   - alternate hopping and freezing,
   - alternate jumping and freezing, and
   - alternate skipping and freezing.

3. The stretch portion of the warm-up can begin by asking students how they can

   - make their bodies taller,

- make their arms reach the ceiling,
- make their arms reach the side walls, and
- make their hands touch their toes and then try to straighten their knees.

ACTIVITY

1. Select and teach three movement skills:
   - Run
   - Slide
   - Twist

2. Introduce and explore an aspect of the movement element of force—strong or weak:
   - Run like a football player.
   - Run like your legs are made from marshmallows.
   - While standing still, make your body look strong.
   - While standing still, make your body look weak.
   - Change the feeling in your muscles to show that they are strong or weak.

3. Develop a small movement pattern using the three movement skills and the movement elements. For example, ask students to slide, twist, and melt down weakly or rise up strongly and run.

COOLDOWN

Depending on how vigorous the class was, choose one of the following:

1. Stand the students in a circle and have them
   - place their arms out or on their hips;
   - put their chins on their chests and breathe deeply, raising their heads as they inhale and lowering their heads as they exhale; and
   - raise their arms up to their sides as they inhale and lower them as they exhale.

2. Discuss the day's activities with students, including what seemed important to them and what they think they should remember.

WARM-UP

1. The lubrication portion of the warm-up should include an inventory of the joints and muscles and an exploration of how they can be moved. Starting with the top of the body, ask the students how many ways they can move
   - their heads and necks;
   - their shoulders;
   - their arms, elbows, and wrists;
   - their torso;
   - their hips and legs; and
   - their knees, ankles, and feet.

   (This exploration can also be done from bottom to top.)

2. The aerobic portion of the warm-up is called "fraction" warm-up because it teaches directional signals using mathematics. Have students face forward, feet comfortably apart. They will change directions every eight counts using small jumps in place and jump turns. The teacher is the caller, and the students jump simultaneously with the call.

   A sample series of calls follows:

Caller (counts aloud)	1, 2, 3, 4, quarter (5), turn (6), to the (7), right (8).
Student	Jumps in place for the eight counts. On the first count of the next eight-count pattern, student executes turn as commanded.
Caller (counts aloud)	1, 2, 3, 4, half (5), turn (6), to the (7), left (8).
Student	Facing new direction, jumps in place for the second eight counts, then executes turn as commanded on the first count of the next eight-count pattern.
Caller (counts aloud)	1, 2, 3, 4, three-quarter (5), turn (6), to the (7), left (8).
Student	Facing new direction, jumps in place for the third eight counts, then executes turn

as commanded on the first count of the next eight-count pattern.

Note: Always continue the activity from the direction that was last called.

This activity, in addition to being aerobic, sharpens listening skills and teaches math skills.

3. Begin the stretch portion of the warm-up by asking students how they can
   - make their bodies taller,
   - make their arms reach the ceiling,
   - make their arms reach the side walls,
   - make their hands touch their toes while they try to straighten their knees, and
   - make their muscles feel and become longer.

     Also ask students how these stretches can be done while sitting or lying on the floor.

ACTIVITY

1. Select and teach three movement skills:
   - Three-step turn
   - Kick
   - Leap

2. Introduce and explore an aspect of the movement element of space—change of direction.

3. Develop a small movement pattern using the three movement skills and the movement element. For example, ask students to do a three-step turn, run and leap, and kick (letting the kick change their direction).

COOLDOWN

Depending on the class activities, choose one or more of the following to be included in your cooldown:

1. Have students do push-ups and crunches/curl downs, trying to exceed their personal best.
2. Have students stand in a circle and
   - place their arms out or on their hips;

- put their chins on their chests and breathe deeply, raising their heads as they inhale and lowering their heads as they exhale;
- raise their arms up to their sides as they inhale and lower them as they exhale; and
- roll the body down to a limp, folded-over position while exhaling and then bring it to an erect, shoulder-squared position while inhaling.

3. Discuss the day's activities with students, including what seemed important to them and what they think they should remember.

Grades 7-12

WARM-UP

1. The lubrication portion of the warm-up includes an inventory of the joints and muscles and an exploration of how they can be moved. Starting with the top of the body, ask the students how many ways they can move
   - their heads and necks;
   - their shoulders;
   - their arms, elbows, and wrists;
   - their torso;
   - their hips and legs; and
   - their knees, ankles, and feet.

   (This exploration can also be done from bottom to top.)

2. The aerobic portion of the warm-up begins by having the students stand in a circle. They then play "follow the leader" with each student developing a movement that he or she feels contributes to the aerobic activity.

3. The stretch portion of the warm-up continues with the students in a circle. They each demonstrate a movement, which the rest of the class follows, that contributes to this section.

ACTIVITY

1. Select and teach three movement skills.
   - Jazz box
   - Kick, ball change

- Wrap turn

2. Introduce and explore the movement element of space—use of floor pattern.

3. Combine movement skills and movement element:
   - Working in small groups have the students create three poses.
   - Combine these poses with the above movement skills.
   - Perform movement patterns in a number of different floor patterns.
   - Present the small group creations to the class.

COOLDOWN

Depending on the class activities, choose any one or more of the following to be included in your cooldown:

1. Have students do push-ups and crunches/curl downs, trying to exceed their personal best.

2. Have students stand in a circle and
   - place their arms out or on their hips;
   - put their chins on their chests and breathe deeply, raising their heads as they inhale and lowering their heads as they exhale;
   - raise their arms up to their sides as they inhale and lower them as they exhale; and
   - roll the body down to a limp, folded-over position while exhaling and then bringing it to an erect, shoulder-squared position while inhaling.

3. Discuss the day's activities with students:
   - What part of the lesson seemed important to them?
   - What do they think they should remember?
   - What did they learn?
   - Which of the movement patterns did they enjoy the most and why?

Three Parts of a Dance

A well-structured dance has a beginning, a middle, and an end.

The Beginning

The beginning of the dance should be clear, and, whatever the choice, should capture audience attention. Some options are to

- think of the opening as a tableau, a picture, or a painting;
- start the dance on stage or off; or
- start the dance with music or without or begin the music before the dance.

The Middle

The middle or body of the dance should not lose the audience by being boring or trite. Among the countless ways to make the middle interesting are to

- vary movement patterns,
- repeat movement patterns,
- perform movement patterns at different times,
- have different groups perform complementary movement patterns simultaneously, or
- vary dancers' positions on the stage.

The End

The conclusion should also be clearly defined:

- If the dance ends "on stage," hold the final pose as though it were a painting.
- Have the dancers leave the stage.
- End the dance with the music, have it continue after the music has ended, or end the dance and have the music continue.

Both teacher and students should look at the dance with an artist's eye. Most people know what looks good, so remember, aesthetics is in the eye of the beholder.

Learner Outcomes and Student Assessment

Evaluating students' classwork is a necessary part of the educational process. Use the following Student Assessment Form, based on the

Student Assessment Form

Name _____ Grade _____

Score _____

Scale: 1-5 5 = Exceptional
3 = Normal for age group
1 = Needs work in this area
NA = Not applicable for this age group

OUTCOMES

Movement skills

1.
2.
3.
4.
5.

*Choreographic/
creative process*

1.
2.
3.
4.
5.

Cognitive skills

1.
2.
3.
4.
5.

Social/aesthetic skills

1.
2.
3.
4.
5.

projected outcomes of each lesson, to make the task easier. Outcomes, or the desired results of any given lesson, include four areas of assessment: movement skills, cognitive skills, choreographic/creative process, and social/aesthetic skills.

Movement skills refer to the student's ability to develop a movement vocabulary composed of specific movement skills and movement elements.

Cognitive skills refer to the student's ability to solve problems and use critical-thinking skills, memorization skills, as well as conceptualization, verbalization, and listening skills.

The choreographic/creative process refers to the student's ability to use movement skills and elements in order to improvise and create choreography.

Social/aesthetic skills refer to the student's ability to work cooperatively, exhibit self-control, and observe and evaluate performances.

Summary

To summarize, you can develop and implement creative lessons as the instructor and/or facilitator. These lessons will provide the student with necessary skills based on learner outcomes. Consider four areas of assessment: movement skills, cognitive skills, choreographic/creative process, and social/aesthetic skills.

PART II

Identifying Building Supplies—Materials and Tools Needed for Building Dances

The following materials are needed to build dances:

- Movement skills
- Movement elements
- Knowledge of historical and social perspectives
- Knowledge of ethnic influences
- Three ways of organizing music

Movement Skills—The Foundation

All movement, from the everyday activity of walking down the street to the skilled moves of an athlete or dancer are either locomotor or nonlocomotor. Locomotor movement takes you from one place to another, whereas nonlocomotor movement is usually centered around the axis of the body. The terms nonlocomotor and axial can also be used interchangeably.

The four basic locomotor movements are

- walking,
- running,
- hopping, and
- jumping.

Other locomotor movements, such as skipping, leaping, galloping, and sliding are combinations of the above movements.

The four basic nonlocomotor movements are

- swinging,
- bending,
- stretching, and
- twisting.

Basic body positions commonly used in physical education classes are also helpful when building dances. They are

- tuck position—lying (front, back, side), standing, or sitting;
- pike position—lying, sitting, or standing;
- layout position—lying (front, back) or standing;
- stride position—standing; and
- straddle position—standing or sitting.

Examples of grade-appropriate movement skills, used alone and in combination, follow. Movements are explained in the glossary and on Deal-a-Dance cards.

Grades K-3

Run	Walk	Skip
Leap	Hop	Jump
Slide	Crawl	Prance

Step, hop	Step, step	Bow
One-footed turn	Gallop	Slither
Stamp	Slap thighs	Arm circle
Sit	Cross legs	Log roll
Step and drag	Kneel—two knees	Lunge
Kneel—one knee	Elbow swing	Kick
Half knee bend	Head roll	Scale
Flexed foot	Extended foot	Attitude
Twist	Arm stretches	March
Stand on balls of feet	Butterfly	Side step

Grades 4-6

Jump turns (quarter, half, three quarter, full)　Wrap turn

Tuck jump	Jazz box	Allemande
Three-step turn	Snap fingers	Lame duck step
Knee turn	Promenade	Pike—jump
Ball change	Pivot turn	Layout—jump
Stride—jump, turning	Straddle—jump	

Grades 7-12

Grapevine	Knee bend	Knee fall
Seat turn	Lame duck turn	Pony
Bell clicks	Leap	Stag jump
Jazz walk	Kick, ball change	Triplet
Scissors jump		

Movement Elements

Change movements by altering the following elements: shape, space, time, and force. These terms are defined as follows:

• **Shape**—the positions and ways a body is used. Alter shape by changing the position of the body and/or body parts. The body can be curved or twisted, angular or straight, symmetrical or asymmetrical.

• **Space**—how and where the movement takes place. Movement can alter the use of space through change of direction (face stage right, face stage left, face upstage, face downstage), change of size (large, small), change of level (lying, sitting, kneeling, standing, elevated), change of floor pattern (circle, half circle, zigzag, diagonal line, straight line), and change of focus (look up, look down, look right, look left, look behind).

• **Time**—the time it takes to do a movement or a movement pattern. Alter time by change of speed (tempo—faster, slower) and change of rhythm.

• **Force**—the quality of the movement. Alter force by change of energy (strong and weak movements), change of quality (suspended, shaking, collapsed, swinging, percussive, and sustained), and change of movement flow (controlled and almost uncontrolled).

Ethnic and Cultural Influences

Dance is for everyone but means different things to different cultures. Dance occurred even in ancient times. It has been used in religious rites and ceremonies, and to many cultures is a rite of passage, thanking of the Gods, or raising and quieting of spirits (see Figure 2.1). Dance is also a way to celebrate, with the movements, meaning, and

Figure 2.1   The adoration of the goddess may bring the much needed rain.

techniques being handed down from one generation to the next. Men dance with men, women dance with women, and men and women dance together.

Students can delve into their ethnic backgrounds and pull movement and material that can be used in building dances. This exploration celebrates ethnic diversity and can be used to integrate dance into the social studies curriculum.

Historical and Social Perspectives

History and social studies classes study how the dances of past and current societies reflect trends and popular cultures of the times. Only in recent times has dance become a social activity, a reflection of social mores and customs often dictated by the music of the day. Such vernacular dance, done to vernacular music, is bound by what popular culture will accept. The young are the experimenters with new dance forms, often to the chagrin of the establishment. The minuet of the French courts (see Figure 2.2) and the waltz of Austria were social

Figure 2.2   By assuming the proper position, dancers can create the impression of a minuet.

dances that had a hard time catching on. The Black Bottom of the Roaring 20s was thought shocking but is now part of history. Likewise, the Watusi from the 1960s is now only nostalgia for those who danced their sneakers off during that period. Of course, all this time the Virginia reel, square and line dancing, and folk dancing from the melting pot of cultures was being kept alive, in strong part by the physical educators and their students.

Dance as a performing art is also recent. The Greeks in ancient times performed their dances in amphitheaters, and in medieval times madrigal dancers entertained in the streets. Ballet developed in Europe, was bandied about, and finally found a base in France; hence the vocabulary of ballet is in French. In the United States, modern dance took hold experimentally, in the early 1900s, with Isadora Duncan. The vocabulary for modern dance was usually in the language of the country where it was being done. However, ballet and modern dance now enjoy a commonality—for example, "tendu" means "point your foot" in any dance form. Tap evolved into a performing art from Black rhythmics and Irish clogging. It is truly an American dance form, along with musical comedy (Broadway show dances) and jazz.

With the emergence of the importance of physical fitness, dance became a physical activity as well as a social one. During a dance workout or class, the muscles, tendons, and ligaments of the body are put to full use, as is the cardiovascular system. Dancing can be a fun way to get in shape and stay fit. Anyone at any age can participate in a dance program as long as it is designed and carried out at an appropriate technical level. Preschoolers learn stretching, hand-eye coordination, and beginning muscle control, and young children add more advanced muscle control and alignment. Teens and young adults learn to refine all those skills and begin to push their bodies' capabilities, aerobically as well as technically. The new concept of dancing for senior citizens includes dance exercises as well as line and square dancing. People of different abilities are being given dance exercises to help keep their bodies in shape and to increase their social interaction. Dance is a social equalizer.

Three Ways of Organizing Music

Music is the mortar that holds dance together. It can be an integral part of creating dances and can greatly influence a piece of choreography. It can also enhance, inspire, encourage, and stimulate the creative process and give dancers a form whereby they can create and remember choreography. Using music fosters organizational skills by compelling the choreographers to think through how the composer uses phrasing, when that phrasing changes, and how it makes them think differently about putting together combinations and repetitions of movements. Organizing the music makes the task of the choreographer more manageable because it breaks a long piece of music into workable sections.

When music is used, the choreography can respond to the feeling, the speed, the rhythm, the phrasing, and/or the words. Following are three ways of organizing music to facilitate its use when building a dance.

Using Verbal Phrases

Using the words from a piece of music is a simple way to approach choreography. The choreographer selects movements that "act out" the words, like with pantomime. For example, you organize the music by individual words, sentences, or verbal phrases (such as "the sky is blue"). If you were using "Rock-a-Bye Baby," you could segment the verbal phrases within the music like so ($\frac{6}{8}$ ♫♫ ♩ ♪):

Section 1: Rock-a-bye baby

Section 2: on the tree top

Section 3: When the wind blows

Section 4: the cradle will rock

Section 5: When the bough breaks

Section 6: the cradle will fall

Section 7: and down will come baby, cradle and all!

You would now be able to work with each section, individually, as a separate thought process.

Counting Beats

Organizing the music by counting beats can also be an effective way of applying music to choreography. Because there are so many styles of music and not everyone is familiar with them all, the examples used are the nursery rhymes "Three Blind Mice" and "This Old Man." What you see in the first two charts are methods of counting beats (quarter notes) and measures (groups of beats) within musical phrases. Since most novice choreographers don't use written music, we've eliminated actual scores of the songs.

What you see are eight measures of four counts each. This eight-measure phrase (32 counts) can be clapped out by the students, one clap per beat or count. Make sure that they clap on a hold or rest even though there may not be a word with that note. Conversely, they shouldn't make a clap for every word. Many times there are several words during one beat.

The method of counting shown for "Three Blind Mice" and "This Old Man" demonstrates where the beats are found. After becoming familiar with the beats in a piece of music, you can then begin the process of organizing it for choreography.

Since most popular music is written in 4/4 time, which means that four quarter notes (♩) equal a measure, the two songs that are used as examples are applicable because they, too, are written in 4/4 time, with four beats to a measure. The music familiar to children is usually repetitious, and movement patterns or sequences can be repeated, matching movement phrases to music phrases. The two choruses of "This Old Man" don't have to be choreographically different. To accent the different words, make two separate moves, one for the words "one" and "thumb" in the first chorus and another for the words "two" and "shoe" in the second chorus.

Grouping Measures

Once you are comfortable with counting beats and identifying measures, you're ready to group the measures into the musical phrasing. One way to clarify this method of organizing music is to compare it with the structure of the English language. Just as words are used to make sentences, and sentences are grouped to make paragraphs, beats are used to make measures and measures are grouped into phrases.

To illustrate the organization of songs for choreography, a slash mark (/) is used to symbolize each measure of four beats. These measures will be grouped on a line to indicate the natural breaks in the musical phrasing, determined by the music, as opposed to verbal phrasing, which is determined by the thoughts expressed by the words. Examples 1 and 2 chart the musical phrasing by keeping the slash marks on a single line for each phrase. Once the music has been charted, each phrase may be addressed individually.

Counting Method—Example 1

Words ▶	Three	Blind	Mice	
Quarter Note ▶	♩	♩	♩	♩
Count ▶	1	2	3	4

Three	Blind	Mice	
♩	♩	♩	♩
1	2	3	4

See	How they	Run	
♩	♩	♩	♩
1	2	3	4

See	How they	Run	
♩	♩	♩	♩
1	2	3	4

They all	ran after	the Farmer's	Wife
♩	♩	♩	♩
1	2	3	4

She Cut off their	Tails with a	Carving	Knife
♩	♩	♩	♩
did 1	2	3	4

you Ever	See such a	Sight in your	Life
♩	♩	♩	♩
1	2	3	4

as Three	Blind	Mice	
♩	♩	♩	♩
1	2	3	4

Words ▶	This	old	Man		He	plays	One
Quarter Note ▶	♩		♩		♩		♩
Count ▶	1		2		3		4

	He	plays	Knickknack	On	my	Thumb
	♩		♩	♩		♩
	1		2	3		4

with a Knickknack	Paddywack	Give the	dog a	Bone
♩	♩	♩		♩
1	2	3		4

This	old	Man	came	Rolling		Home
♩		♩		♩		♩
1		2		3		4

This	old	Man		He	plays	Two
♩		♩		♩		♩
1		2		3		4

He	plays	Knickknack	On	my	Shoe
♩		♩	♩		♩
1		2	3		4

with a Knickknack	Paddywack	Give the dog a Bone
♩	♩	♩ ♩
1	2	3 4

This	old	Man	came	Rolling		Home
♩		♩		♩		♩
1		2		3		4

Three Blind Mice

Lyrics/Phrases	"/" = 4 $\downarrow$ (beat)
Three blind mice, three blind mice	/ /
See how they run, See how they run	/ /
They all ran after the farmer's wife	/ / /
She cut off their tails with a carving knife	
Did you ever see such a sight in your life	
As three blind mice	/

Your chart should look like this:

Phrase 1	/ /	total of eight counts (or two 4s)
Phrase 2	/ /	total of eight counts (or two 4s)
Phrase 3	/ / /	total of 12 counts (or three 4s)
Phrase 4	/	total of four counts

This Old Man

Lyrics/Phrases	"/" = 4 ♩ (beat)
This old man, he plays one	/ /
He plays knickknack on my thumb	
With a knickknack paddywack	/ /
give the dog a bone	
This old man came rolling home	
This old man, he plays two	/ /
He plays knickknack on my shoe	
With a knickknack paddywack	/ /
give the dog a bone	
This old man came rolling home	

Your chart should look like this:

Phrase 1	/ /	total of eight counts (or two 4s)
Phrase 2	/ /	total of eight counts (or two 4s)
Phrase 3	/ /	total of eight counts (or two 4s)
Phrase 4	/ /	total of eight counts (or two 4s)

You can teach these three methods of counting and organizing music to students. Ask students to bring in some of their favorite pieces of music, one of which is selected by the class. The class listens to the music and identifies the rhythmical pattern by clapping out the beat. Using a chalkboard or drawing paper, make a chart following the examples above. Now begin the process of choreography. Again, addressing one phrase at a time simplifies the task. Having the students bring in current popular music to be used for choreography also increases their enthusiasm for dance. This music tends to be easy to work with because it is thematic and repetitious, with phrasing that follows definite patterns. However, because of copyright laws you can't use an illustrated charting of an existing recording. Therefore example 3 is a format that is similar to today's popular music. Some choreographers organize their music in groups of eight counts. This means that they use two measures of four counts to equal one slash mark, which reflects eight counts. The chart uses this method.

Grouping Measures—Example 3

Any popular song

Introduction	/ / / /
Theme A	/ / /
	/ /
Theme B	/ / / /
Transition	/ /
Chorus	/ / / /
Theme A	/ / /
	/ /
Theme B	/ / / /
Transition	/ /
Chorus	/ / / /
Theme C	/ / / /
	/ / / /
	/ / / /
Theme A	/ / /
	/ fades out

Slash (/) equals eight counts

Summary

Understanding how movement skills and elements can be used to build dances gives you a basic knowledge of the origin of all movement. Also, understanding the social, cultural, and historical significance of dance gives additional material to use when creating dances. Finally, using music to frame a dance can be simple, once you learn how to organize and approach it.

Constructing the Frame and Roof–Meaningful Organization of Materials

ow that the materials to compose dances have been as-sembled, it is time to get down to the nuts and bolts of organizing these materials. This section of the book will guide the reader through various ways to structure dances, uses of dance to portray a story line, and fun ways to use props and sound.

Structure and Choreographic Forms

You can structure dances in several ways. Often they are structured by music, and many terms for dance forms are taken from music terminology. Whether or not music is actually used, however, is irrelevant to the structuring of choreographic forms.

Four of the most popularly used choreographic forms are canon or round, A B A, rondo, and theme and variation.

Canon

Using a canon or round is like singing "row, row, row your boat" in parts but using movement in place of or along with lyrics. This structure works well with young as well as older children because of the small amount of material to remember and the familiarity of this musical pattern. Also, a little choreography goes a long way, that is, one movement pattern is repeated continually.

Movement Example

The class will learn the following 12-count (beat) combination, which has been divided into three 4-count phrases.

(First phrase) Walk forward four times (count 1, 2, 3, 4).

(Second phrase) Walk backwards four times (count 1, 2, 3, 4).

(Third phrase) Squat down (count 1), hold (count 2), stand (count 3), clap (count 4).

Next, divide the class into three groups and arrange them in scattered formation across the room. Group 1 is over to the right, Group 2 is center, and Group 3 is over to the left.

- Group 1 begins the first four counts while Groups 2 and 3 remain motionless.
- As Group 1 starts the second four counts, Group 2 begins the first four. Group 3 is still motionless.
- As Group 1 starts the third four counts, Group 2 begins the second four, and Group 3 begins the first four.
- Each group stops after completing the entire 12-count combination three times in a row (36 counts in all). As groups finish, they should remain motionless until all groups have completed their 36 counts.

Variations

Notice how the dances are affected when you modify them in some of the following ways:

- Use two groups instead of three.
- Begin the canon with Group 1 on the left, 2 in the center, and 3 on the right.
- Arrange the groups from front to back with Group 1 across the front, Group 2 across the middle, and Group 3 across the back.
- Reverse and begin back to front.
- Mix students from Groups 1, 2, and 3 so they are not standing next to anyone from their own group. Begin the canon with the students of Group 1, then 2, then 3, making sure that the students are aware of space and spatial relationships because they will be moving forward, backward, and up and down at the same time, while working next to each other.
- Start the combination with all groups moving in unison (all 36 counts). Repeat the combination in canon. When all groups have completed their 36 counts, the entire class repeats the combination in unison. Canons look best when sections of movements are largely contrasted.

A B A

The A B A format includes a movement phrase (A), a new movement phrase (B), and a return to the first movement phrase (A).

Movement Example

Ask your students to do the following movements.

(A) Run across the floor, rotate two times, and then look at the audience.
(B) Kneel slowly looking down at floor, searching for something, then rise up quickly.
(A) Run across the floor, rotate two times, and then look at the audience.

Variations

- Class performs in unison.
- Class is divided into two groups, one that does the A movement pattern each time it happens and the other the B movement pattern.
- Class is divided into three groups, one that does the first A, one that does the B, and a third that does the second A.

Rondo

A rondo can be described as A B A C A D A. The choreographic pattern is A, the primary movement pattern, alternating with B, C, and D, which are different from A.

Movement Example

(A) Arms overhead, out to sides, in to waist, and down.

(B) March in place.

(A) Arms overhead, out to sides, in to waist, and down.

(C) Four quick leaps across the floor.

(A) Arms overhead, out to sides, in to waist, and down.

(D) Run in a circle.

(A) Arms overhead, out to sides, in to waist, and down.

Variations

- One group of students performs A and freezes while other students perform B, C, and D.
- Students perform with their backs to the audience.
- A shorter dance can be created by performing A, B, A, C, A.

Theme and Variation

The theme and variation format is a movement pattern with subsequent pattern variations of the original: A, A1, A2, A3.

Movement Example

(A) Walk forward eight times.

(A1) Walk forward eight times while waving arms above head.

(A2) Walk forward eight times while clapping hands.

(A3) Walk forward eight times while bent over.

Characterization and Story Line

Characterization is the backbone of dances that have a story line and of dances that show people interacting. Whenever a choreographer has to tell a story or bring a character to life, the image portrayed is a personal interpretation of what is in the choreographer's frame of reference. Students can use brainstorming techniques to develop the qualities of a character and the movements that might portray these qualities. This interpretation can be literal or abstract.

Movement Example

Start with the following story line:

Goldilocks encounters the three bears and is frightened.

- In a literal interpretation, dancers would explore movements that they feel best express Goldilocks' actual reactions. (She could put her hands on her cheeks and pull back as if holding her breath.)
- In an abstract interpretation, the action would be more metaphorical. For example, the dancers might express a quality of fear. (She could be skipping around and suddenly freeze, staring off into space.)

You can also base story lines on an actual piece of literature, a student-developed original story, or a collaborative effort between students and teacher. The story line can be the basis of one dance or an entire show, and you can use music and/or narration to enhance the story or make it easier to interpret.

Sounds and Props

Responding to sounds adds depth and dimension to choreography. A fun option to the use of recorded music is to have a class make their own in the form of assorted rhythm instruments, homemade instruments, percussive clapping, slapping and snapping of various parts of the body, or vocal noises. The "music" can be performed by the dancers or by a different set of children as accompaniment to the dancers.

Movement Examples

- Use the sounds of tearing paper, a bicycle horn, and a slide whistle. For each sound, create a movement and perform it to that sound.

- As students are walking have them freeze in a pose on a single clap, change direction on the sound of a finger snap, and continue walking on a double clap.

The theatrical term "props" comes from the word properties. Actors would use a glass, flower, book, chair, hat, cane, etc. Dancers can also use props to add interest and different qualities to dance movement. For example, the hats that the dancers use in the finale of "A Chorus Line" add emphasis and establish a distinctive style to the choreography (see Figure 3.1). Developing movements, attitudes, and characters through the use of props can be a fun and interesting exercise.

Figure 3.1   You don't need glitzy costumes to convey the aloof air of "A Chorus Line."

Movement Examples

- Have all students in a dance about rowing use oars, incorporating the use of the oars in the actual movement.
- Have students wearing tissue boxes painted yellow on their heads create "a yellow brick road" (see Figure 3.2).

Figure 3.2   Using inexpensive props can easily portray an idea.

Summary

A knowledge of choreographic forms is needed when assembling material into a dance. These forms provide a structure for the material. Choreographic forms include the canon or round, the A B A format, the rondo, and the theme and variation format. Each form can be explored, providing countless possibilities.

The use of characterization is essential to dances with a story line. Students can use brainstorming techniques to develop movements which portray characters. The interpretation can be literal or abstract. The use of sounds and props will add further dimensions to your choreographic endeavors.

PART IV

Adding Architectural Details—Individualization of Dances

A dditional aspects of dance can enhance creativity and help deliver the choreographic message to the audience. Consider the following when choreographing:

- Accenting
- Use of gestures
- Stylizing
- Use of expressive quality

Accents—Adding Emphasis

Accenting choreography is not the same as accenting in music. Accenting choreography makes a section of a movement pattern stronger, adds interest, and highlights a particular moment in the music. An accent occurs when a move is made bolder, when the surprise of a sharp move is interjected in a slow section, or when a position is held for an extra amount of time.

Additionally, accenting (making stronger) a different beat in each measure adds variety, as follows:

First Measure **1** 2 3 4
Second Measure 1 **2** 3 4
Third Measure 1 2 **3** 4
Fourth Measure 1 2 3 **4**

When performing this 16-count walking combination, the dancer would perform a stamp on the bold number. Students can play around with this concept by clapping as well as walking. Some could clap as an accompaniment as others walk. At times, only the accent beat needs to be clapped.

Gestures—Telling the Story Through Movement

Gestures are valuable tools in getting a message across from the dancer to the audience. They include movements of the body, head, arms, hands, or face that express an idea, opinion, emotion, etc. Gestures, for example, are an important component of many folk and ethnic dance forms, and the art of pantomime uses gestures exclusively, going from one to the next to tell a story or portray a thought.

Stylizing—Creating a Place and Time

There is a difference between style and stylizing. For example, the names of choreographers or famous dancers bring a particular style to mind. In ballet, it is George Balanchine and Enrico Cecchetti; in modern dance, Martha Graham and Merce Cunningham; in tap, Fred

Astaire and Gregory Hines, and in jazz, Bob Fosse. The term stylized, however, refers to a dance being done with the flavor of a country, a vernacular dance (dance from a specific social era, such as the Charleston, minuet, cabbage patch, or break dancing), or one of the formal dance disciplines. It doesn't have to be technically or traditionally correct or historically accurate (see Figure 4.1). What's important is the impression it gives the audience. An example of stylization is the dance sequence "America" from *West Side Story*, in which the dancers aren't actually doing the dances of Puerto Rico but are giving the impression of that country with a turn of the wrist and a flick of the hip. They are also responding to the cultural flavor of the music.

Figure 4.1   Choreography need not be authentic to give the impression of time and place.

Expressive Qualities—Creating Moods Through Movement

Expressive qualities are essential within dances that have a theme or story line. Changes in facial expressions enhance gestures, but that is only part of the picture. Expressive qualities are displayed in the total body, for example, as shown in Figure 4.2, the body slumps over and shows fatigue, sadness, or dejection. Students can interact, displaying their fears, anger, frustrations, and hope. Dance allows students to express their emotions in a nonthreatening and accepting atmosphere.

Figure 4.2   When the body is slumped and the face is looking at the floor, the audience will feel the loss.

Summary

Providing the finishing touches on dances can make the difference between a series of movements that are merely joined together and a well-rounded dance piece that makes a personal statement. The effective use of accents, gestures, stylizing, and expressive qualities can provide those finishing touches.

PART V

Putting It All Together—
Build a Dance in 7 Steps:
The Choreographic Process

utting it all together is as easy as stepping 1, 2, 3, 4, 5, 6, 7. The steps are as follows:

1. Choose subject matter.
2. Explore and select movements.
3. Coordinate music and movements.
4. Explore possibilities.
5. Refine and memorize choreography.
6. Add finishing touches.
7. Perform choreography.

Just follow these seven easy steps, and voilà—you have a dance.

Step 1—Choose Subject Matter

Decide on a story line, theme, or topic, and, if applicable, music for your dance.

Step 2—Explore and Select Movements

Explore movements based on the subject matter through a creative process or by combining basic movement and dance skills.

Step 3—Coordinate Music and Movements

If used, music should be organized by using verbal phrasing or counting of beats as described in Part II—Three Ways of Organizing Music. Combinations of movements can be put to the phrases as follows, using "This Old Man" or almost any popular song. The following organization of music uses the counting of beats, and the movement patterns use combinations of basic movements.

This Old Man

Phrase	Choreography
1	Step hop, step hop (beats 1, 2, 3, 4)
	Step, 2 claps, hold (beats 1, 2, 3, 4)
2	Step, kick, step, kick (beats 1, 2, 3, 4)
	Step, kick, stamp, hold (beats 1, 2, 3, 4)
3	Spin on one foot (beats 1, 2), two jumps (3, 4)
	Four claps on thighs (beats 1, 2, 3, 4)
4	Four runs (beats 1, 2, 3, 4)
	Three runs (beats 1, 2, 3), kneel on one knee with arms reaching out (beat 4)

Almost Any Popular Song

Phrase	**Choreography**

Introduction

1-4   Dancers begin in a scattered formation.

1. (First eight) Stand straddle, hands on shoulders; hold eight counts.
2. (Second eight) Squat down, with head down, hands on floor; hold eight counts.
3. (Third eight) Head looks at audience; hold eight counts.
4. (Fourth eight) Slowly rise up, in seven counts; strike any pose on count 8.

Theme A

1-3

1. Walk three steps forward; clap on count 4; walk three backward; clap on count 8.
2. Walk to the side, three steps to the right; clap on count 4; reverse.
3. Make four poses; hold each pose for two counts.

4-5   4-5. Walk for 16 counts, around and through neighbors in a scattered formation (like a busy street scene).

Theme B

1-4   Repeat the introduction.

Transition

1-2   1-2. Take 16 counts to form two concentric circles.

Chorus

1-4

1. Inside circle jogs clockwise eight counts; outside circle jogs counterclockwise eight counts.
2. Reverse.
3. Take four counts; all converge to center forming one large cluster; all face audience on counts 5-8.
4. Use eight counts to jog back to original scattered formation.

Theme A
   1-5   Repeat theme A.

Theme B
   1-4   Repeat theme B.

Transition
   1-2   Repeat transition.

  Chorus
   1-2   Repeat chorus.

Theme C
  1-12   1-11. Repeat the first three 8s of theme A as a three-part canon.

                      12. Walk around and through neighbors in a scattered formation for eight counts.

Theme A
   1-3   Repeat theme A.

   4-5   Walk scattered and leave the stage as the music fades.

Rock-a-Bye Baby is an example of choreography set to verbal phrasing.

Rock-a-Bye Baby

Section 1
Choreography

Rock-a-bye baby
Cradle arms while swinging them to right and left.

Section 2
Choreography

on the tree top
Turn and face the back with arms lifted and fingers spread out.

Section 3
Choreography

When the wind blows
Sway body right and left in the same position as above.

Section 4
Choreography

the cradle will rock
Turn to front with arms in cradle position and sway right and left.

Section 5
Choreography

When the bough breaks
Reach out and clap hands on word "breaks."

Section 6
Choreography

the cradle will fall
Body "melts" down; end sitting on floor.

Section 7
Choreography

and down will come baby, cradle and all!
Reach arms up to "catch" baby and pull arms into lap.

Use a combination of these two organizational methods when choreographing. Combining methods allows you to emphasize a particular word or phrase within the music.

When you add music to the creative process of building a dance, you have a medium that holds the layers of bricks together. Music supports and beautifies the basic elements of dance and adds interest to the total impact.

Step 4—Explore Possibilities

You can alter and enhance choreography by changes and variations of level, focus, direction, rhythm, floor pattern, and placement of dancers. Level, focus, direction, and floor patterns are addressed in Part II under Movement Elements. You can alter a single movement or an entire movement pattern by changing any of the movement elements.

Rhythm Changes

Change of rhythm results from varying the way you use counts. Look at how many ways you can change a simple walking pattern. The walks in each of the following four-beat measures are changed as indicated.

- Take four steps (one movement per beat).

step	step	step	step
1 (♩)	2 (♩)	3 (♩)	4 (♩)

- Take two steps (holding one beat after each step).

step	hold	step	hold
1 (♩)	2 (♩)	3 (♩)	4 (♩)

- Take one step (hold for three additional beats).

step	hold	hold	hold
1 (♩)	2 (♩)	3 (♩)	4 (♩)

- Take five steps (first three on beats 1 & 2, the next two on beats 3, 4)

step	step	step	step	step
1 (♪)	& (♪)	2 (♩)	3 (♩)	4 (♩)

- Take eight steps (& 1 & 2 & 3 & 4). This pattern is called double time.

step	step	step	step	step	step	step	step
1 (♪)	& (♪)	2 (♪)	& (♪)	3 (♪)	& (♪)	4 (♪)	& (♪)

Formation Changes

The use of different formations can frame, highlight, and add interest to the choreography. Formation refers to the placement of dancers on the stage. Though not directly related to formations, stage directions are important because they establish a common reference point. They should be learned by all age groups to facilitate the giving and understanding of directional instructions (see Figure 5.1).

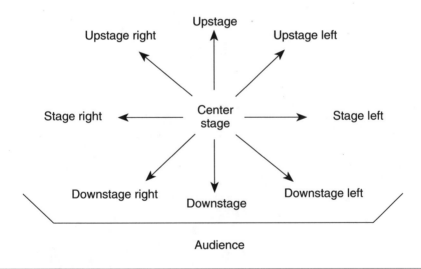

Figure 5.1   Stage directions.

Figure 5.2 shows sample formations that may be used to group dancers. These formations can be used while dancers are stationary or moving and may be changed many times during a dance. Groups of formations can perform individually or in unison. A layering of movements within the formations creates an additional effect.

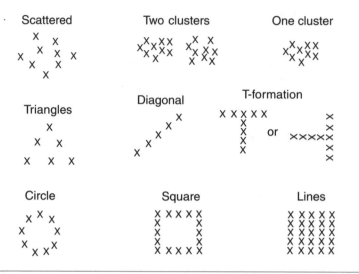

Figure 5.2   Sample formations.

Formation Example 1

While in a scattered formation the front half of the group kneels and waves their hands while the back half stands and steps side to side (see Figure 5.3).

Figure 5.3   Layering movements can create an additional effect.

Formation Example 2

The group condenses to a huddle as in football with bodies hunched together in a tight circle. They may have arms around each other or pulled into their center (see Figure 5.4).

Figure 5.4 A football huddle formation shows unity.

Formation Example 3

Experiment with a pyramid, as used in gymnastics or cheerleading. Divide group so that the largest number and strongest people are at the base. People can be standing or on their hands and knees. The next group, fewer in number, get onto either the shoulders or the backs of the base people. End with one person on top (see Figure 5.5).

Step 5—Refine and Memorize Choreography

Make sure that all dancers are performing the movement sequences as choreographed and make corrections before the errors become learned behavior. Once the dance has been "cleaned up," rehearse it, rehearse it, and rehearse it again. The "body" must learn the dance so that if stage fright occurs muscle memory takes over.

Figure 5.5   A pyramid formation shows strength and balance.

Step 6—Add Finishing Touches

Performing a dance is more than just walking through the choreography. Dancers shouldn't hold back but perform the choreography "full-out." They need to smile, acknowledge the audience, exude energy, and execute every movement to its fullest—in other words, have "stage presence." Costumes can range from simple to elaborate depending on budget and availability. Whether the costumes are the coordination of street clothing, a simple t-shirt, or an elaborate outfit ordered from a catalogue, costumes make the dance special and thus make the students feel special. No matter how simple or inexpensive, costumes should be a part of every performance.

Lighting and scenery are a wonderful addition to any performance but not always necessary or available. Set pieces can be a collaborative effort with the visual art department and are alternatives to a full set. If stage lighting is not available, a simple on-and-off to blackout will establish some desired effects.

Step 7—Perform the Choreography

Once you have refined and practiced the choreography and added the finishing touches, the piece is ready to perform. Whether the performance is in an informal setting, such as a gymnasium or multipurpose room, or in a traditional auditorium with a stage, the students will revel in the thrill of performing. They can perform for their peers, for younger children, or for their parents and community members. Once your troupe of dancers has the confidence, and you are sure they are up to it, you can volunteer their services to local community functions. If you have several classes in which you work out choreographic problems and build dances, you will have enough material to do a concert on your own, or you can collaborate with the music person to do a joint concert.

Summary

Creating a dance can be as simple as the seven steps. By taking one step at a time the creative process will be far less threatening or difficult, and by building one dance at a time you can reach the goal of constructing an entire dance concert.

PART VI

Inspecting Your Creation– The New Building: Observation to Assessment

During a performance the person viewing the dance piece can observe and assess individual dancers, individual pieces of choreography, and the performance as a whole. Have students view live or videotape concerts performed by professionals as a means of comparison (see Figure 6.1). This type of assessment is not only important for the evaluation process but also for making adaptations, changes, and improvements for the future. Students are capable of assessing both peer and professional performances.

Figure 6.1   Viewing live performances is a vital part of the learning experience.

Assessing Student Performance

A videotape of students' performance can be a valuable tool for documenting your program as well as for assessment. The students can use the videotape to assess themselves and their peers, and you can use it when evaluating a student. Use the following form after viewing a live performance or a videotape. It was developed with input from students, who gave the criteria they felt were important for a successful performance. This form can be adapted to any situation by getting additional input from your students to make it relevant to them and their performance. Ask the students to rank each item on the form using a scale of five to one, five being the best and one being the least.

Student Performance Assessment Form

Name _____   Total score _____

Rate the individual above using the following scale:

> **Scale: 1-5**   5 = Always
> 4 = Most of the time
> 3 = Can improve
> 2 = Needs much improvement
> 1 = Really bad
> NA = Not applicable
> DK = Do not know

Throughout the performance the performer listed above

_____ 1. Stayed in character.

_____ 2. Showed energy.

_____ 3. Looked at audience when appropriate.

_____ 4. Smiled when appropriate.

_____ 5. Covered up mistakes well.

_____ 6. Reacted well to technical difficulties.

_____ 7. Looked out at audience (not down).

_____ 8. Obeyed performance rules (did not touch costume, hair, face, wear jewelry, etc.) while performing.

_____ 9. Used proper facial expressions.

_____ 10. Held endings.

_____ 11. Acted seriously about the concert.

_____ 12. Acted appropriately during performance (no talking, laughing, or horseplay).

_____ 13. Obeyed safety rules (no gum chewing, no touching backstage equipment).

_____ 14. Remained calm before, during, and after performing.

_____ 15. Was quiet in the wings.

_____ 16. Made exits and entrances on time.

_____ 17. Made movements big.

_____ 18. Performed choreography as it was choreographed.

_____ 19. Kept in time with the music.

_____ 20. Executed the dance movements correctly.

_____ 21. Reacted well to accents within the music.

_____ 22. Was conscious of spacing concerns during show.

During rehearsal, class, and backstage:

_____ 23. Worked cooperatively with group.

_____ 24. Followed through on costume responsibilities.

_____ 25. Rehearsed as if it were a real performance.

_____ 26. Was quiet.

_____ 27. Was generally cooperative.

_____ 28. Was respectful to teachers (did not have to be spoken to).

_____ 29. Contributed to the smooth running of the show by not touching costumes and/or props belonging to someone else.

_____ 30. Made quick changes effectively.

_____ 31. Was ready to perform on time.

_____ 32. Listened and obeyed all instructions.

_____ 33. Obeyed all rehearsal and classroom safety and etiquette (no chewing gum, no sitting down during class, no talking during class, no horseplay).

_____ 34. Was helpful in organizing before and after performances.

_____ 35. Helped classmates during show.

Assessing Professional Performance

Use the following forms when assessing video/live professional performances. The forms, which are grade-appropriate, contain criteria needed to make an evaluation.

Performance Critique for Grades K-6

Staging/Choreography

1. Look for the area of the stage where most of the performing was done. Was it on the sides, middle, or close to the front or back?
2. Did the dancers use all of the floor space?
3. What dance movements did you recognize?
4. Describe your favorite movement.

Costumes

1. Look for costumes that you like. Describe one. What colors did you notice in the costumes?

Lighting

1. What lighting changes did you notice?
2. Were the lights always white, or did they change color, and what colors did you see?

Your Feelings

1. Did the dancers look like they were having a good time?
2. Were their faces happy or sad?
3. Do you think any of the pieces were too long? Too short?
4. What piece did you like the best?

Exercise

On a separate piece of paper do the following:

1. Choose two pieces (or two dancers) and tell how they were alike or different.
2. With your class discuss your own thoughts about the performance.

Performance Critique for Grades 7-12

Choreography/Staging

1. Did the dancers use the whole stage or did they generally remain in one particular area of the stage?
2. What area of the stage seemed to catch your attention the most? The downstage? Stage left? Stage right? Upstage?
3. Did the movement change levels? Did the dancers go down to the floor? Were there any lifts?
4. Did the movement look difficult to do? Did the movement look simple? What made it look difficult or simple?
5. Describe your favorite movement.

Music

1. Did the music enhance or detract from the choreography?
2. Did the choreography use the music? Did the dancers use the music?

Performance Quality

1. What were the facial expressions on the dancers? Did the facial expressions help you understand the piece?
2. Were the dancers focused on what they were doing?

Costumes

1. Did they catch your eye? Were they boring?
2. Did they seem to restrict the dancers in their movement? Were they easy to move in?

Lighting

1. Were the dancers in enough light, or were they hard to see?
2. Did the lighting change throughout the performance, or did it remain the same?
3. If you noticed changes in the lighting, what were they? How did the changes enhance the performance?

Your Observations

1. Was the performance too long? Too short?
2. What dance techniques did you recognize? Were they from ballet? Modern? Jazz? Other?
3. What was the audience reaction?
4. What stood out most about the dancers? The choreography? The performance?

Exercise

1. Compare and contrast two pieces that you enjoyed the most.
2. Discuss your own thoughts and feelings on the performance in writing. Share your thoughts with others.

Summary

Students need the opportunity to express how they feel about a piece of art, whether it is a piece created and performed by professionals or by themselves or their peers. The student performance assessment and performance critique forms can help facilitate this.

PART VII

Building Dances From Sample Blueprints— Activities to Implement the Choreographic Process

The following nine dance-building activities have been designed for several purposes. Each is a learning experience, using basic skills and concepts, and a fun activity designed to be nonthreatening to both teacher and student. Each encourages some aspect of the creative process and makes the teacher a facilitator rather than a demonstrator.

DANCE-BUILDING ACTIVITIES	Page

Each dance activity has sections labeled description of activity/procedure; example activity; grade-appropriate adaptations; and learner outcomes/student assessment. These sections guide you through the activity to maximize its use. Communicating with students is also a constant source of inspiration. Their willingness to cooperate and bring their thoughts and ideas to the class make every day a rewarding, exciting, and fulfilling experience.

Deal-a-Dance

This activity increases movement skills and movement vocabulary through the use of the enclosed 112 playing cards that are printed on both sides. Each card has two different movement skills or concepts for a total of 224 movement examples. Four types of cards facilitate the creation of movement patterns or pieces of choreography. This activity can be either teacher-facilitated, student-directed, or both. You may use these cards for only one class lesson or to build an entire unit.

Description of Activity/Procedure

There are four categories of cards:

Dance Technique

The 84 pink movement-example cards within the Dance Technique and Basic Movement category each have a different dance or movement term, a definition of that term, and suggested ways to vary it, called the "Try this" section.

Sports and Game Movements

Each of the 52 blue movement-example cards displays a different sport or game skill, which students are asked to imitate. This category gives the nondancer a user-friendly approach to dance. Many sport and game movements have a direct correlation to dance movements, and because both adults and children are more familiar with sports and games than dance, this category provides a comfortable way to explore choreography. Included are variations of how to move beyond the skill level and incorporate it into dance. Students need not perform the skill to perfection but merely stylize it for use in building a dance. A definition has thus not been included, only some safety tips in the "Try this" section.

Elements That Change Movements

The 56 green movement-example cards address movement concepts and other factors that can alter a movement or a series of movements. These cards are subcategorized as follows: change of focus, change of level, change of quality, change of floor pattern, change of direction, change of mood, change of energy, change of flow of movement, change of speed, and change of rhythm. Included are a variety of circumstances to help students visualize the listed element.

Creative Movement Suggestions

The 32 yellow movement-example cards can help younger children be creative through guided exploration. The "Try this" section includes situations to help stimulate ideas on how to make their bodies move in different ways. These cards are actually effective with all age groups, including adults.

Ways to Use the Cards

A sample card is shown in Figure 7.1, with the various parts labeled. The cards can be used in the following ways.

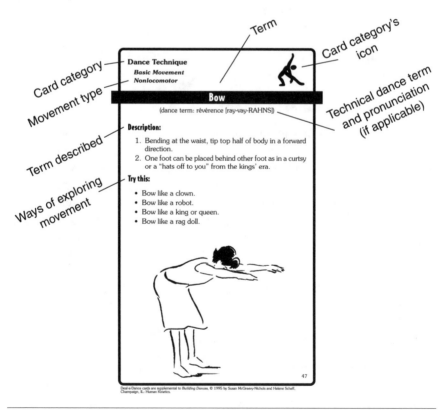

Figure 7.1   A sample dance card.

Select a certain number of cards from each category and combine them to create a movement pattern or dance. The class can work on a dance as a whole, in small groups, or individually. Specific cards can be selected by the teacher or students or randomly chosen by either. Music may or may not be used. Part III contains information on how to create dances and should be used in conjunction with this activity.

- Teach two to three movement skills per lesson, working towards building a bigger dance and movement vocabulary.
- Experiment with the "Try this" section.
- Combine the skills or variations of the skills.
- Organize students in groups of three to five. Give each group a number of cards and have them arrange them in an order. They can lay the cards out on the floor in front of them and try different arrangements. Once the students decide on an order, they should link the movements from each card. Transitions can be accomplished by adding additional movements or simply moving from one to the next. They should clearly define the beginning and end of their sequence by freezing the starting position of the first movement and holding the finish of the last movement. The groups can then perform their "dances" for each other.
- A specified number of counts (beats) can be assigned to each movement or to the entire sequence of movements.
- To add music to this activity, teach the class to clap out a beat and organize the musical selection for use when choreographing.
- Select a subcategory from the element cards, such as change of focus. Pull all the cards in that subcategory (look up, look down, look right, look left, perform two different focus changes in a row, look around, and look behind). Then plan a lesson around this concept, exploring how changing the focus gives different meaning and emphasis to movement. You can use this method in conjunction with a card from Dance Technique and Basic Movement or Sports and Game Movements.
- Have the class do any combination in a canon.

Example Activity

This example guides the entire class through the creative process of building a piece of choreography. To start, select four cards for the lesson from only two of the categories. They are

Dance Technique and Basic Movement

Three-step turn

Jazz box

Clap

Sports and Game Movements

Karate kick

Read The definition on the card to the students. Next, read the definition again slowly and ask the students to try the movement as it is being read. This activity will improve their listening skills and not put you on the spot to demonstrate (see Figure 7.2). Once the students have familiarized themselves with the four movements, explore the "Try this" section of the cards. Next, with input from the class, decide on an order for the movements and what transition movements will be needed, if any. Students then learn and practice the sequence (movement pattern). Once they have mastered the sequence to the best of their capacity, select another card from the Elements That Change Movements category. Encourage students to discuss how the information on this card can vary the dance sequence that's already been established.

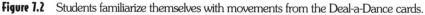

Figure 7.2   Students familiarize themselves with movements from the Deal-a-Dance cards.

Let's say you and the class have built the following combination:

1. Three-step turn to the right, touch the left foot in
2. Jazz box ending with a
3. Karate kick and then
4. Clap three times

This combination is done with each step taking one count (beat), using 12 counts in all. Using an additional 12 counts, this combination can now be reversed. This 24-count phrase can be done to music. Adding an Elements That Change Movements (change of focus) card, namely "looking up," the group could decide to look up when doing the touch in, on the karate kick, and/or on the last clap. You could then divide the class in two groups, having half observe while the other half performs. The observers could be invited to comment on how the change of focus makes the dance sequence different, makes it more interesting, or perhaps gives the choreography an "air," "attitude," or style. Similarly, the Suggestions for Creative Movement card can be introduced and used. For example, if the term *crash* is selected, they could do the entire combination with their heads looking up so that they would crash into each other because they couldn't see where they were going. You could also discuss other variations from the "Try this" section.

Grade-Appropriate Adaptations

Deal-a-Dance can be adapted to any age level by varying the presentation and organization of the material. Suggestions for modifications follow.

Grades K-3

The range of this age group's selection should be limited. Still, children this age enjoy a challenge. (Too many times educators use the excuse that children in these grades are neither experienced enough nor capable of grasping or developing ideas and concepts. Nothing could be farther from the truth.) You merely have to organize the material differently and be organized yourself. It is best to teach one skill at a time to the entire group and have the class determine which of the learned skills will be performed in what order.

Grades 4-6

The children in this age group are very creative, motivated, and capable. They aren't afraid to experiment with any ideas presented to them, and they often have ideas of their own to contribute. They can work with the cards in small groups of three to five children and begin to experiment with choreographic forms.

Grades 7-12

These students can be the most reluctant, for they yield to peer pressure and are self-conscious despite having great ability. Your challenge is to make the class feel comfortable about themselves and the subject matter and present Deal-a-Dance in a nonthreatening, nonjudgmental, and fun atmosphere. Students in these grades are capable of working on their own and should be experimenting with different music, seeing how it affects their choreography.

Learner Outcomes/Student Assessment

The Deal-a-Dance activity should achieve the following desired outcomes.

Movement Skills

Students should be able to

- demonstrate nonlocomotor movements to a rhythmical beat,
- demonstrate locomotor movements to a rhythmical beat,
- identify a beat in a variety of music,
- understand and demonstrate elements that can change movement,
- demonstrate basic dance techniques,
- combine a series of movements to form movement patterns, and
- demonstrate an increased skill level.

Cognitive Skills

Students should be able to

- remember a sequence of movement,
- focus on task and give positive input,

- apply decision-making skills,
- describe dance in appropriate dance terms,
- identify movement and movement elements occurring in a movement pattern or dance,
- identify choreographic concepts and form, and
- recall movement patterns learned during a previous class.

Choreographic/Creative Process

Students should be able to

- vary combination through improvisation,
- apply music to combination,
- demonstrate a knowledge of choreographic forms,
- apply choreographic and movement skills to express ideas nonverbally through dance,
- demonstrate how to vary choreography using elements that can change movement, and
- demonstrate innovation and creativity while exploring movement.

Social/Aesthetic Skills

Students should be able to

- demonstrate self-direction and self-discipline,
- contribute to the group effort in an interested, positive manner,
- perform the finished combination or dance,
- watch others perform and provide constructive criticism,
- work effectively in a small group, and
- have fun and show satisfaction with accomplishments.

When assessing the student, base your assessment for this activity on the outcomes and use the sample student assessment form.

Picture Dance

This activity can heighten visual interpretation and observation skills. The process of the activity also builds self-esteem while encouraging teamwork and allows children with limited English verbal skills to participate with peers.

Description of Activity/Procedure

The activity uses pictures as a source for the positions/movements used in creating dances. The images are imitated by the individual or group. Several of these "pictures" are then linked with movement to create movement patterns or small dances. The first step in this activity is to gather pictures from magazines, newspapers, old programs, brochures, etc. The teacher could have the raw materials on hand or encourage the students to bring them to school. The pictures should be of people in action—dancers, athletes, or anyone who moves.

Next, the students select (or are assigned) a group of pictures. They can work individually or in small groups to establish a picture order. Then the students, alone or with help from you, mimic the images in the pictures and, using the creative process, link the individual images by connecting movements. Music could enhance the whole project, adding another dimension to the creative process.

Example Activity

A group of five children selects three pictures—one a baseball player swinging a bat, another a horse leaping high over a hurdle, and the last a person bending over a flower bed. The order that the group decides on is

1. bending,
2. batting, and
3. leaping.

In a cooperative effort, the group first bends over, then starts to rise while twisting their bodies as if to swing a bat, then ends the sequence with their version of the horse in midair (see Figure 7.3). Encourage the group to elaborate on their actions, adding linking movements to make the sequence a beginning piece of choreography.

Figure 7.3   In a Picture Dance activity, students imitate visual images and develop transitions.

Grade-Appropriate Adaptations

Picture Dance can be adapted to any age level by varying the presentation and organization of the material. Suggestions for modifications follow.

Grades K-3

With you facilitating, students work collectively to imitate or mimic the images in the pictures. Their imitations will be very literal. Also encourage them to explore the various ways they can go from one image to another.

Grades 4-6

Students this age are capable of working in larger groups and with more pictures. You can give them a specified number of counts in which to accomplish each position and movement and an appropriate time frame for the linking moves. Encourage them to use the elements of choreography to vary the sequence, such as adding arm movements to the bending over, a swing as the batting twist is approached, and a quick run before the leap.

Grades 7-12

Students can take the elements used in grades 4-6 and begin to develop a story line around them, adding moves as warranted. They could also choose music and make the sequence fit the musical phrasing or make the quality of the movements fit the mood of the music (lyrical, staccato, heavy, light, etc.).

Learner Outcomes/Student Assessments

As a result of the Picture Dance activity students can achieve the following desired outcomes.

Movement Skills

Students should be able to

- simulate an image or picture,
- choose an order and link pictures with movement,
- notice and give attention to details within the movement or movement pattern,
- understand and demonstrate movement elements and skills,
- demonstrate an increased skill level, and
- combine series of movements to form movement patterns.

Cognitive Skills

Students should be able to

- demonstrate observation skills,
- recall a sequence of movements,
- focus on a task and give positive input, and
- apply decision-making skills.

Choreographic/Creative Process

Students should be able to

- demonstrate innovation and creativity while exploring movement and
- apply music to movement patterns.

Social/Aesthetic Skills

Students should be able to

- demonstrate self-direction and self-discipline,
- contribute to the group effort in an interested, positive manner,
- perform the finished combination or dance,
- watch others perform and provide constructive criticism,
- work effectively in a small group, and
- have fun and show satisfaction with accomplishments.

Base your assessment for this activity on the outcomes and use the sample student assessment form.

Words, Sentences, and Paragraphs

This activity lends itself to team teaching with the literacy, English, or bilingual teacher. The activity is a wonderful bridge between native languages and English in schools where children are bilingual or have few English language skills, and in situations where students have poor language skills, it can help raise the literacy level by introducing concepts through a fun, nonthreatening activity. For young students with preverbal skills, the activity also furnishes a means of expression.

Description of Activity/Procedure

A dance or sport movement is assigned a specific word, either in English or the student's native language. These individual words are then linked together to form a sentence, and sentences are linked to form a paragraph.

Example Activity

Let's say "The sky is blue!" is the lead sentence in what is to become a paragraph. Figure 7.4 illustrates children performing the movements for this opening sentence. The move represented by the word "sky" is a standing layout. The word "is" is a standing straddle with hands on hips, and the move represented by "blue" is a tuck (squat). The moves can then be performed in tandem.

The next sentence is "The blue sky turns dark when it is going to rain." Again "blue" is a tuck (the student can stay in the position from the previous sentence or rise and tuck again); "sky" is a standing layout; "turns" is a two-revolution rotation; "dark" is a stride position with hands over face; "going" is a run; and "rain" is a leap.

The closing sentence is "The rain from the dark sky makes the flowers grow." Once again, "rain" is a leap; "from" is a pulling in of arms to chest; "dark" is the stride position with hands over face; "sky" is a standing layout; "makes" is a clap; "flowers" is a kneel on one foot with arms stretched overhead; and "grow" is a slow rise. This sentence marks the end of the paragraph.

You read the paragraph, and the students perform the appropriate movements for each word. This activity provides a progression of both thought and movement. The sentence is factual, so learning is

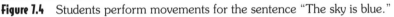

Figure 7.4 Students perform movements for the sentence "The sky is blue."

taking place, and as words from one sentence are carried into the other, a feeling of continuity and movement results.

Grade-Appropriate Adaptations

Words, Sentences, and Paragraphs can be adapted to any age level by varying the presentation and organization of the material. Suggestions for modifications follow.

Grades K-3

You might try some of the following modifications:

- Groups of students portray different words.
- Students develop simple sentences.
- Students choose movements for words.

Grades 4-6

One modification is to line students up in rows and then group them. Each group represents a specific word in the paragraph. As the paragraph is being read, the members of each group execute their word, holding a position after they move. Students must not move when it is not their word. Also the action should move from left to right and from top to bottom as when one reads. An example follows:

Group 1	Group 2	Group 3		Group 3	Group 1
The	"sky"	"is"	"blue."	The	"blue"	"sky"

Group 4	Group 5			Group 6		Group 7
"turns"	"dark"	when	it is	"going"	to	"rain."

Group 7	Group 8		Group 5	Group 1	Group 9
The	"rain"	"from"	the	"dark"	"sky"	"makes"

Group 4	Group 5
the	"flowers"	"grow."

Another modification is to use movements as punctuation marks, which are added to the paragraph.

Grades 7-12

Ask students to create a short story using movements.

Learned Outcomes/Student Assessment

As a result of the Words, Sentences, and Paragraphs activity students can achieve the following desired outcomes.

Movement Skills

Students should be able to

- translate words into movement
- increase personal movement vocabulary,
- combine series of movements to form movement patterns,
- demonstrate an increased skill level, and
- understand and demonstrate movement elements and skills.

Cognitive Skills

Students should be able to

- recall a sequence of movement patterns,
- focus on a task and give positive input,
- understand simple sentence structure, and
- understand paragraph structure.

Choreographic/Creative Process

Students should be able to

- create movements which portray words, thoughts, and ideas; and
- demonstrate innovation and creativity while exploring movement.

Social/Aesthetic Skills

Students should be able to

- demonstrate self-direction and self-discipline;
- contribute to the group effort in an interested, positive manner;
- perform the finished combination or dance;
- watch others perform and provide constructive criticism;
- work effectively in a small group; and
- have fun and show satisfaction with accomplishments.

Base your assessment for this activity on the outcomes and use the sample student assessment form.

Story Dance

This activity contributes to the development of nonverbal communication and the ability to develop story lines. It can also create opportunities for team teaching and be a means of collaborative teaching with you taking part in the planning. Children at any age level can create their own story from simple facts you give them. You could also choose a theme, such as "Taking a Trip" or "Saving Our Oceans." We've included suggestions for ways to build a story based on a theme. For example, meet with the English teacher and learn what literature the children are reading while you are doing this unit. From "Mrs. Popper's Penguins" in the elementary grades to "Little House on the Prairie" in the middle grades or "Romeo and Juliet" and "Old Man and the Sea" in the upper grades, the challenge of bringing these pieces of literature to life nonverbally is exciting. This project is also an ongoing one that enhances memory as well as interpretive skills.

One way of enticing children to think about the project from one class period to the next is to make the story grow each time. The children can add new dimensions and twists to the stories they create. The possibilities are endless.

Description of Activity/Procedure

Portray a story, either existing or original, through movement. For this activity, someone supplies a story that is age-appropriate and of interest to the students, who then read the story or have it read to them. Through a series of movements, mime, and feelings, they should depict the story nonverbally, working independently or as teams. They are to create movement patterns and combination steps that help them to relate the story to their "listeners."

Students are eager and capable of doing their own research on a given theme, and an effective method for drawing information and ideas from children is brainstorming, an exciting process for both students and teacher. Give the students subcategories within a theme, for example, "Saving Our Oceans." The subcategories might be jobs, fun things to do, and sea life. The children then, as quickly as they can, shout out words and phrases within a specific subcategory. Record the suggestions on a blackboard or an easel pad so that all the students can see and more easily remember what has already been suggested. Limit brainstorming sessions to five-minute periods, and explain that the "shouting out" part of this exercise is acceptable in this situation, though not always acceptable in a regular classroom setting. These ideas can then be explored in a number of ways through movement.

Example Activity:
"Goldilocks and the Three Bears"

Team effort: Three people are chosen or volunteer to be the bears and one, Goldilocks. You may want to pick names out of a hat to be fair. You or the team decides which version of the story is to be told. Figure 7.5 shows students depicting a critical moment in the plot through movement.

The children decide which movement skills would best depict the Papa Bear, the Mama Bear, and the Baby Bear—maybe the baby would skip, the Mama would take light and delicate steps, and the papa, big, heavy, plodding steps. They could then go through the motions of going out into the forest for a picnic or a walk while the porridge cools. They could incorporate movements done in a circle or use a blanket as a prop, raising and lowering it as part of the preparation for the picnic.

Figure 7.5   Students perform "Goldilocks and the Three Bears" as a Story Dance.

Meanwhile, Goldilocks would enter the scene. She could be frightened (cautious lunging steps) or exhilarated by the fresh air and take skipping, jumping, and leaping steps until she discovers the home of the three bears. Her focus would then be that of investigation and discovery—tasting, trying the chairs, and finally going to bed and sleep. She could use stretches, extended movements, and slow motion to depict fatigue.

The bears reenter and discover the half-eaten cereal, the broken chair, and finally the guest in the bed. All the movement patterns could be decided by the children, or, depending on the situation, you could give direct input. Though this example is simplistic, considerable leeway exists for more creativity in the Story Telling activity.

All of these verbal exercises now translate into movement patterns and eventually into a story ballet. (A story ballet doesn't mean that the dance discipline need be ballet. All dances that tell a story are called ballets.)

Grade-Appropriate Variations

Story Dance can be adapted to any age level by varying the presentation and organization of the material. Suggestions for modifications follow.

Grades K-3

The students can decide on a theme, with the research done for them or done as a team effort between teacher and students. They can then take the facts and begin to put them in a logical order with help from you. The students can make up several endings, with you guiding them through a movement pattern that tells the story.

Grades 4-6

Discuss the "serial" and "cliff hanger" methods of story telling, for example, the soap opera. The story/dance should be developed in such a way that it can be performed in segments using, for example, a narrator, pleading with the audience to "stay tuned for the next exciting episode."

Grades 7-12

Students in these grades can come up with their own theme or story line. The story-building can be done in collaboration with any of the academic or arts teachers, giving the whole unit a broader scope. In addition to the above-mentioned skills, the children also learn to do research.

Learned Outcomes/Student Assessment

Story Dance should result in the following desired outcomes.

Movement Skills

Students should be able to

- convey a story line through movement,
- increase personal movement vocabulary,
- combine series of movements to form movement patterns,
- demonstrate an increased skills level, and
- demonstrate an understanding of how to use the body as an instrument for expression and communication.

Cognitive Skills

Students should be able to

- recall a sequence of movement patterns;
- focus on a task and give positive input;
- effectively use brainstorming techniques;
- demonstrate an understanding for research skills; and
- research, write, and present.

Choreographic/Creative Process

Students should be able to

- create movements which portray words, thoughts, and ideas;
- demonstrate innovation and creativity while exploring movement;
- create and perform dances based on their own ideas;
- apply choreographic concepts to express ideas nonverbally, through dance; and
- create and develop a story line.

Social/Aesthetic Skills

Students should be able to

- demonstrate self-direction and self-discipline;
- contribute to the group effort in an interested, positive manner;
- perform the finished combination or dance;
- watch others perform and provide constructive criticism;
- work effectively in a small group; and
- have fun and show satisfaction with accomplishments.

Base your assessment for this activity on the outcomes and use the sample student assessment form.

Write What I See

This activity hones observation and listening skills while enhancing literacy skills.

Description of Activity/Procedure

A student assumes a position while others accurately describe that position in writing. A student who did not see it then recreates the position based on the written description.

Establish two sets of teams and place them in opposite areas of the room. One individual from each team assumes a pose, and the other students on that team describe the pose in writing exactly as they see it. This written description can be in a listed or paragraph form.

The teams swap writing descriptions, which are then read by one student while another on the team tries to recreate it.

Example Activity

Child A stands in a scale position on the right foot with the left leg stretched out behind, the knee straight, and foot extended. The arms are in front of the body, with elbows bent at a 90-degree angle and palms facing up. The head is lifted to the ceiling. Child B writes that Child A is standing on one foot; the other leg is behind. The arms are bent. (See Figure 7.6.)

While this is taking place, Child C and D are doing the same thing. Team 1 (A and B) and Team 2 (C and D) then swap written descriptions. Child C reads Team 1's description to Child D, who tries to reenact the original position of Child A based on what is being read. All students sit and watch, and you then ask the child who was the original demonstrator if the position being shown is correct. If it is not accurate then he or she should demonstrate exactly how it should look. You then discuss with the class how the written description must be altered and elaborated on to match the original pose.

Grade-Appropriate Adaptations

Write What I See can be adapted to any age level by varying the presentation and organization of the material. Suggestions for modifications follow.

Figure 7.6   In a "Write What I See" activity, students write descriptions of poses.

Grades K-3

Because of limitations to their writing skills students could tell what they observed while you record what they say on a blackboard or easel pad. Have one child leave the room or go to the other side of the room with their back turned while this activity is going on. The child is then invited back, and the description read while the child recreates it. The group makes corrections as a whole, and you discuss vocabulary and the importance of being specific about "What I See."

Grades 4-6

Basically, these students would follow the example. You should place greater emphasis on written skills such as grammar and punctuation, and at the end of class, have students link poses to make a movement pattern.

Grades 7-12

Students can split into groups of three consisting of a recorder, a describer, and a demonstrator. Each group does the exercise and then trades off with another team.

For these older students, you should place a greater emphasis on vocabulary, grammar, and sentence structure. Also, have the groups link all poses to create a class dance.

Learner Outcomes/Student Assessment

As a result of the Write What I See activity, students can achieve the following desired outcomes.

Movement Skills

Students should be able to

- increase personal movement vocabulary,
- notice and give attention to details within the movement or movement pattern,
- understand and demonstrate movement elements and skills, and
- demonstrate an increased skill level.

Cognitive Skills

Students should be able to

- demonstrate observation skills,
- recall a sequence of movements,
- focus on a task and give positive input,
- apply decision-making skills,
- show an improvement in listening skills, and
- show an improvement in writing skills.

Choreographic/Creative Process

Students should be able to

- create a movement pattern using a series of positions.

Social/Aesthetic Skills

Students should be able to

- demonstrate self-direction and self-discipline;
- contribute to the group effort in an interested, positive manner;
- perform the finished combination or dance;

- watch others perform and provide constructive criticism;
- work effectively in a small group; and
- have fun and show satisfaction with accomplishments.

Base your assessment for this activity on the outcomes and use the sample student assessment form.

Machine Dance

This activity helps develop conceptualization skills while increasing spatial and kinesthetic awareness. It also enhances the creative process through problem solving, team work, and cooperative thinking.

Description of Activity/Procedure

Groups of students recreate a machine using the concept of gears and action/reaction. For this activity the students need to come up with a "machine," either real or imagined. Divide the class into working groups of three to five students. Odd numbers seem to work the best. The groups can all decide on one machine, or each group can develop one on its own.

Using their bodies, students create the parts of the machine. They then need to show how one "gear" is dependent on another to work. One child starts by moving the part that links to the next child and then the next, etc. When each group has completed the task, you can then link all the groups around the perimeter of the room making one gigantic automation.

Example Activity

Student A stands with both hands on hips, facing forward. His right arm swings across his chest, turning him one half revolution to the left, where he taps the shoulder of Student B, who was standing with his back towards the front of the room. Student B bends in half from the waist, sending his right arm to the side, where it touches the head of Student C, who is sitting on the floor, all curled up, with his back to Student B. Student C, when tapped on the head, unfolds, stretching his arms and legs out to either side, where they make contact with Students D and E, who then do a forward roll at the same time but in different directions (see Figure 7.7).

To take this one step further, as you add students you can eventually return to the first person, who starts the sequence over from the beginning. You can also add a "problem" to the task by asking the students to handle a prop while passing it through the machine.

To take it even further, you can add music. The students will then have the added job of making their moves fit the rhythm or beat of the

Figure 7.1   In a Machine Dance, students interact like moving parts of a machine.

music. By changing the music the students will find that their "machine" may act very differently.

Grade-Appropriate Adaptations

Machine Dance can be adapted to any age level by varying the presentation and organization of the material. Suggestions for modifications follow.

Grades K-3

You or an older student helper would need to create several "gear" moves and demonstrate a few of these to the class. The class would then be asked how they would connect these moves. They could each choose one of the gears they wanted to be, and the machine would work in a circle so they could see each other. They could also make a field trip to a watch hospital, automatic car wash, or bottling plant so that they could actually watch gears in action.

Grades 4-6

This age group would be more knowledgeable about gears and would happily come up with real and imagined machines. A good reference point for them would be "Charlie and the Chocolate Factory." They could also make a field trip to an automobile assembly line or a factory that used robotics to assemble a product.

Grades 7-12

This age group could build a dance based on a project from their physics or science class, or they could observe an actual machine in motion. They could then analyze the different parts, seeing what makes them work and how they work. Their bodies would simulate those parts, acting and interacting with other parts to recreate the working machine they saw.

Learner Outcomes/Student Assessment

As a result of the Machine Dance activity students can achieve the following desired outcomes.

Movement Skills

Students should be able to

- simulate an image,
- choose an order and link images with movement,
- notice and give attention to details within the movement or movement pattern,
- understand and demonstrate movement elements and skills,
- demonstrate an increased skills level,
- combine a series of movements to form movement patterns, and
- increase personal movement vocabulary.

Cognitive Skills

Students should be able to

- demonstrate observation skills,
- recall a sequence of movements,
- focus on a task and give positive input, and
- apply decision-making skills.

Choreographic/Creative Process

Students should be able to

- demonstrate innovation and creativity while exploring movement, and
- apply music to movement patterns.

Social/Aesthetic Skills

Students should be able to

- demonstrate self-direction and self-discipline;
- contribute to the group effort in an interested, positive manner;
- perform the finished combination or dance;
- watch others perform and provide constructive criticism;
- work effectively in a small group; and
- have fun and show satisfaction with accomplishments.

Base your assessment for this activity on the outcomes and use the sample student assessment form.

Prop Dance

This activity helps children realize that people are different from their images by having them finish such questions as "A motorcycle jacket means the person in it acts . . .?" or "A velvet hat with a feather means the person wearing it thinks . . .?" While the activity develops creative thinking and observation skills, it also gives the students self-confidence in making decisions and makes them aware of their capabilities. On a social note: We as a society tend to prejudge people based on their actions and clothes. We might predetermine that someone in overalls won't like opera or someone who drives a hot rod cannot possibly be a bank executive. This activity helps students at all levels debate these preconceptions. Prop Dance uses a form of improvisation and helps children with development of a character. They act out what they feel about people who look a certain way and how they think people perceive the character they are portraying.

Description of Activity/Procedure

Students select props that inspire them to create a character through movement. For this activity you need to have a "bag of tricks"—a collection of various hats, scarves, jackets, jewelry, accessories, books, writing implements, purses, pocket "things," etc. The first time around, have the children choose one or two articles from the bag and ask them to create a character from these props. They can write down the characteristics or just keep them in their heads. Have them tell you about the person they are creating then move as they believe their character would.

The next step is to have these characters interact. They can develop a situation and resolve it through dance and movement.

Example Activity

Johnny chooses a baseball cap and a stop watch. He puts the cap on backwards with the beak down against his neck. He puts the stopwatch cord around his wrist and the watch in the palm of his hand. He thus "becomes" a game manager—tough at every angle and precise to the extreme. He develops moves that are forceful, angular, and exacting (see Figure 7.8).

Figure 7.8   Props help convey character.

Tina chooses a sequin tiara and boa. She wraps the boa around her neck and tilts her head into the air. She takes on the air of a showgirl—sophisticated, arrogant, self-controlled, and mildly self-conscious. She parades around the room, strutting her stuff but really worried about what the public will think of her. These two could then develop a problem that would cause them to interact. Maybe they could switch props and empathize with the other's problems.

Grade-Appropriate Adaptations

Prop Dances can be adapted to any age level by varying the presentation and organization of the material. Suggestions for modifications follow.

Grades K-3

Have the children get into a circle. Place a prop in the center and have them all react to it either one at a time or collectively. This age group loses control easily and having them in a circle helps keep them focused. Asking students to freeze so that you can regroup them and regain their attention can also be effective with this age group.

Grades 4-6

Students in this age group can begin to work independently and are not terribly self-conscious. The more outlandish the prop, the more creative they seem to be. After the children are comfortable with the activity, you can do the choosing for them. Selecting props that are not necessarily within their frame of reference broadens their thinking and encourages them to explore new feelings and images for the characters behind the props.

Grades 7-12

Have the students think of and demonstrate traits and characteristics of a person they have in mind, using some of the skills they developed through Deal-a-Dance. Let them tell you what props they need to make the characterization clearer.

You could also add the element of music. Each character freezes "on stage" while one does the dance. You can change the music for each character or have them react to the same music but in the way they believe their character would. After each of the characters is introduced, they could also interact.

Learner Outcomes/Student Assessment

As a result of the Prop Dance students can achieve the following desired outcomes.

Movement Skills

Students should be able to

- demonstrate an understanding of how to use the body as an instrument for expression and communication through movement,
- notice and give attention to details within the movement or movement pattern,
- understand and demonstrate movement elements and skills,
- demonstrate an increased skill level,
- combine a series of movements to form movement patterns, and
- increase personal movement vocabulary.

Cognitive Skills

Students should be able to

- demonstrate observation skills,
- recall a sequence of movements,
- focus on a task and give positive input, and
- apply decision-making skills.

Choreographic/Creative Process

Students should be able to

- demonstrate innovation and creativity while exploring movement,
- apply music to movement patterns, and
- apply choreographic and movement skills to express ideas nonverbally in dance.

Social/Aesthetic Skills

Students should be able to

- demonstrate self-direction and self-discipline;
- contribute to the group effort in an interested, positive manner;
- perform the finished combination or dance;
- watch others perform and provide constructive criticism;
- work effectively in a small group;
- have fun and show satisfaction with accomplishments; and
- express ideas and emotions without being self-conscious.

Base your assessment for this activity on the outcomes and use the sample student assessment form.

Decode-a-Dance

Decode-a-Dance develops interpretation skills both from body language to the spoken or written word and from mind to body to paper. It will increase appreciation of music and how different kinds of music enhance expression. Having older students help the younger ones fosters a cooperative learning experience and develops role models.

Description of Activity/Procedure

An untitled piece (dance) is performed. The students who are observing write a narrative of their interpretation of what the dance means. This decoding can yield different meanings from different people.

For this activity, one student will need to have a vision of a dance or a concept of the desired end result. This person, the choreographer, creates a "sentence, paragraph, or entire story" using dance and movement vocabulary. Several students could take part. The other students become the observers, "decoding" the story as it evolves. They can describe actions, feelings, relationships, etc. As the scene is developed and refined, the choreographer could choose appropriate music, and the observers could comment on how the music helped or hindered the dance concept.

Example Activity

Three students are "on stage," and one is sitting all curled up, as in Figure 7.9. The second student begins to do "shivers" and "shakes," moving the arms as if to get warmer. The third student "blows in" on the scene with a flurry and lands on the curled-up student. The students observing develop the following scenario: A snowball sits on the ground. The "flapping" student symbolizes the cold. The third student is more snow landing on the snowball and making it larger.

Grade-Appropriate Adaptations

Decode-a-Dance can be adapted to any age level by varying the presentation and organization of the material. Suggestions for modifications follow.

Figure 7.9   Choreography for a snow scene.

Grades K-3

You could have an older class of observers tell the performing class of K-3 what they believe the scene depicts. They could also be asked to write it out and compare all the versions that were "seen." They then explain and describe the scene to the K-3 class. The older students could also discuss and demonstrate how dance movements would tell the story. Conversely, the K-3 class could observe an older class and, using verbal skills, tell what the scene meant to them.

Grades 4-6

One half of the class could write out the version of the scene being performed by the other half, thereby "decoding" what they see.

Grades 7-12

An English class can be the forum to introduce critique skills. Critique forms can be found in Part VI.

Learner Outcomes/Student Assessment

As a result of the Decode-a-Dance activity students can achieve the following desired outcomes.

Movement Skills

Students should be able to

- demonstrate an understanding of how to use the body as an instrument for expression and communication through movement,
- notice and give attention to details within the movement or movement pattern,
- understand and demonstrate movement elements and skills,
- demonstrate an increased skill level,
- combine a series of movements to form movement patterns, and
- increase personal movement vocabulary.

Cognitive Skills

Students should be able to

- demonstrate observation skills,
- recall a sequence of movements,
- focus on a task and give positive input,
- apply decision-making skills,
- translate movement into words, and
- show an understanding of what is happening in a dance.

Choreographic/Creative Process

Students should be able to

- demonstrate innovation and creativity while exploring movement and
- interpret choreographic concepts and movement skills used to express ideas nonverbally through dance.

Social/Aesthetic Skills

Students should be able to

- demonstrate self-direction and self-discipline;
- contribute to the group effort in an interested, positive manner;
- perform the finished combination or dance;
- watch others perform and provide constructive criticism;
- work effectively in a small group; and
- have fun and show satisfaction with accomplishments.

Base your assessment for this activity on the outcomes and use the sample student assessment form.

Create-a-Culture

Create-a-Culture teaches interviewing, research, and interpersonal communications skills. Students learn what culture is and begin to have an understanding of what cultural diversity is about and how it positively influences our lives. They also learn ethnic/folk dance skills. This activity is a perfect vehicle for team teaching, and students and teachers in social studies, bilingual, and English classes would be able to make great contributions.

Description of Activity/Procedure

The class as a whole creates a fictitious culture and then creates a dance that this culture might do.

Creating the Culture

Ask students to define culture and describe the components that make up a culture, such as religion, environment, diet, and customs. They then research different cultures and cultural dance forms, their structures, and what the movements represent. Also ask them to interview family or community members who might be knowledgeable about dances and dance movements within their own cultures. Students then share the information, giving the class an understanding of what culture is. Finally, the class creates a fictitious culture, either individually, by groups, or as a class project.

Creating the Dance

Identify the purpose of the dance in the fictitious culture. For example, is it a harvest, rain, celebration, or perhaps rite of passage dance? Then make up movements that represent the type of dance to be created. Once a structure is decided on, have the class order movements within the structure, and perform the dance.

Example Activity

The created culture is from an island with a hot and dry climate. The people are physically small and strictly vegetarians. The soil is poor and not conducive to agriculture, and a staple of their diet is a large fruit that is picked from a tree. In order to eat this fruit, the people have to break it open by pounding it on the rocks.

The dance created is a harvest dance. The people are placed in a circle, and the movements to depict the harvest are reaching to pick, pounding on the rocks, thanking the gods, and eating (see Figure 7.10).

Figure 7.10   A Create-a-Culture harvest dance.

Grade-Appropriate Adaptations

Create-a-Culture can be adapted to any age level by varying the presentation and organization of the material. Suggestions for modifications follow.

Grades K-3

Have the students talk about their individual cultures, including when and why they dance in that culture. You could also introduce a folk tale and create a dance to go with some event in the story.

Grades 4-6

You might choose what event this dance represents, for example, celebration, harvest, etc. Then create movements that represent activities being done during that event, such as worshipping, gathering food, or the birth of a child. You could also create the aspects of the culture that influence the event, such as climate, religion, customs, and food.

Grades 7-12

Create a culture to be part of an international festival of diversity. Students design costumes, bring recipes that they have developed for this culture, invent a language, and create artifacts and music for the culture. They then perform a dance or series of dances based on this created culture.

Learner Outcomes/Student Assessment

As a result of the Create-a-Culture activity students can achieve the following desired outcomes.

Movement Skills

Students should be able to

- demonstrate an understanding of how to use the body as an instrument for expression and communication through movement,
- notice and give attention to details within the movement or movement pattern,
- understand and demonstrate movement elements and skills,
- demonstrate an increased skill level,
- combine a series of movements to form movement patterns,
- increase personal movement vocabulary,
- convey a story line through movement,
- vary the quality of movement through change of expression, and
- learn a dance outside of class to share with the other students.

Cognitive Skills

Students should be able to

- demonstrate observation skills;
- recall a sequence of movements;
- focus on a task and give positive input;
- apply decision-making skills;
- translate movement into words;

- show an understanding of what is happening in a dance;
- effectively use interviewing techniques;
- research, write, and present; and
- demonstrate an understanding of a culture and how it is influenced by climate, religion, customs, and diet.

Choreographic/Creative Process

Students should be able to

- demonstrate innovation and creativity while exploring movement;
- interpret choreographic concepts used to express ideas nonverbally through dance;
- create movements that portray words, thoughts, and ideas;
- create a fictitious culture; and
- create and perform dances based on their own ideas.

Social/Aesthetic Skills

Students should be able to

- demonstrate self-direction and self-discipline;
- contribute to the group effort in an interested, positive manner;
- perform the finished combination or dance;
- watch others perform and provide constructive criticism;
- work effectively in a small group;
- have fun and show satisfaction with accomplishments;
- be more self-confident;
- demonstrate an increased cultural awareness;
- accept others of different backgrounds; and
- show an appreciation of others' abilities and feelings.

Base your assessment for this activity on the outcomes and use the sample student assessment form.

Summary

Although the activities in this part introduce the basics of choreography, they are by no means comprehensive. However, they should give students an appreciation of the bigger picture of dance education. In many cases the activity may be the spark that ignites the flame of curiosity, making a student more likely to seek formal, intensive, and long term dance education.

Glossary

In many instances the terms for dance steps and movement skills are different while the actual steps and procedures are similar. This glossary introduces these steps and skills with everyday terms but also includes correct dance terms and pronunciation. Familiarity with these terms can become part of class vocabulary.

Foot Positions (General Dance) (see Figure G.1)

Figure G.1 Foot positions: (a) first, (b) second, and (c) fourth.

first position—Feet are parallel and slightly apart.

second position—Feet are parallel and about a foot-width apart.

fourth position—Feet are parallel, one foot ahead of the other and about a foot-width apart.

Foot Positions (Ballet) (see Figure G.2)

first position—Heels touch. Toes are turned out. The aim is to make a straight line with the feet though this is not possible at first.

second position—Heels are about 12 inches apart; toes turned out, and weight evenly distributed on each foot.

third position—Feet are touching, heel of right foot in front of arch of left foot, toes turned out. Position can also be reversed.

Figure G.2   Ballet foot positions: (a) first, (b) second, (c) third, (d) fourth, and (e) fifth.

fourth position—Right foot is about 10 inches in front of left foot, hips aligned and facing forward, toes turned out. Position can also be reversed.

fifth position—Feet are touching, heel of right foot in front of left toe, toes turned out. Position can also be reversed.

Arm Positions (Ballet)

first position—Arms are rounded and low beside your body.

second position—Arms are up just below shoulder level and to the sides of your body.

third position—One arm is rounded in front of your body, and the other is extended to the side, as in second position. The arm in front of your body can be at any level.

fourth position—One arm is rounded above your head, and the other is rounded in front of your body.

fifth position—Both arms are rounded and almost touching. They can be low, just below shoulder level, or over your head.

Body Positions

The following are basic body positions for dance, gymnastics, and general physical education. They can be used in building a dance, warm-up and cooldown, starting positions, or general exercise.

flat back—Used in modern and jazz disciplines. Feet are parallel and slightly apart. Body is at a 90-degree angle to the legs, bending from the hips, with no curve of the spine (also called a pike position) (see Figure G.3).

layout—Stand with feet together and arms stretched overhead. Body and elbows straight.

lunge—Legs are in a stride stance. One leg is lifted behind your body, knee straight and toe pointed. The arms can be in any prescribed position (see Figure G.4).

scale or **arabesque**—One leg is lifted behind your body, knee straight and toe pointed. The arms can be in any prescribed position.

stag—Lift one leg to the front, side, or back, keeping the knee bent at a right angle (also called an attitude position) (see Figure G.5).

straddle—Stand with both feet on the floor in a parallel position in a wide stance.

stride—Feet are in a stationary walking position.

tuck—Knees and chest are against each other.

Dance-Building Movements

The following terms are used when building a dance or executing a warm-up, either supported at a barre or unsupported in the center of the room. If a wall-mounted or a portable barre is not available, then the back of a chair or a waist-high ledge can also be used for support.

accented ankle beats without extensions or **battement battu** [baht-MAHN ba-TEW]—Same as ankle beats without extensions, accenting with the working leg pausing either in front or in back.

ankle beats without extensions or **battement serré** [baht-MAHN seh-RAY]—With your foot at the top of the ankle of the supporting

Figure G.3 Flat back.

Figure G.4 Lunge.

Figure G.5   Attitude or stag.

Figure G.6   Circle move of the leg.

leg (sur le coup de-pied), move the leg from front of the ankle to the back. This movement can be done quickly, but the knee must remain turned out.

arm movements or **port de bras** [paur duh brah]—Carrying of the arms, usually involving the body bending and stretching forward, side, or back.

circle move of the leg or **rond de jambe à terre** [rawn duh zhahm ah TEHR]—This exercise helps your leg turn out at the hip joint. Your body and supporting leg should remain still while your working leg moves around to the back in a half-circle pattern with the leg fully extended and the toe fully pointed (see Figure G.6). For outside (en dehors), start with the leg moving forward first and then around in the half circle. For inside (en dedans), start with the leg moving behind and then out to the side and around to the front.

double strike or **double frappé** [frah-PAY]—Same as strike except that the working leg beats around the ankle before it extends out. Starting from back to front or vice versa, the working heel touches the ankle of the supporting leg twice before it extends out.

foot brush or **battement dégagé** [baht-MAHN day-ga-ZHAY] or **glissé** [glee-SAY]—This move is basically the same as pointed foot except that the foot leaves the floor, and it is all done rather sharply.

full-knee bend or **grand plié** [grahnd plee-AY]—Bend your knees as in a half-knee bend, keeping your heels on the ground as long as possible and then letting them lift off. Come up and back to the original position. In second position, your heels stay on the ground, and you do not go all the way down (see Figure G.7). *Note:* Student should assume correct posture with spine aligned. As the knees bend and the body lowers the student should carry the weight in the thighs and should not "sink" to the floor. The buttocks should not come to rest on the heels and calves. When beginning the rise out of the bend, the heels should be pushed down firmly, again placing the weight in the thighs. The back should be straight. This method takes all strain off the knee joint. Very young children do not have the musculature to execute this properly, therefore the teaching of a deep-knee bend or grand plié should not begin until the child is approximately 8 years old.

half-knee bend or **demi-plié** [duh-MEE plee-AY]—Bend your knees sideways over your toes and move back to your original position. Your heels should stay on the ground, and the movement should be as smooth as possible.

kick, **leg raise**, or **grand battement** [grahnd bat-MAHN]—The leg is thrown up (kick) to front, side, or back. It goes through the extended point (tendu [tahn-DEW]) position on the way up and on the way down. The knee is straight and the toe extended in a pointed position. The foot may flex after it has left the floor (see Figure G.8).

pointed foot or **battement tendu** [baht-MAHN tahn-DEW]—Slide your foot along the floor from first or fifth position to an extended point to the front, side, or back (devant, à la seconde, or derriere). Then slide it back to the original position. The tip of the big toe should not leave the floor.

Figure G.7 Pliés: (a) full and (b) half.

rise or **relevé** [ruh-leh-VAY]—Rising up to half-toe (demi-pointe) in any position either on one foot or two.

stable ankle beats or **petit battement** [puh-TEE baht-MAHN]—Same as accented ankle beats without extensions except that the toe of the working leg only taps in front of the ankle of the supporting leg. There is no action from the knee up, and the working ankle is stable.

strike or **battement frappé** [baht-MAHN frah-PAY]—This exercise strengthens your leg and foot. Starting with the heel of the working leg placed above the ankle of the supporting leg (sur le coup de-pied), strike the floor with the ball of your working leg, extending the leg fully with a pointed toe. Return the foot to the original position, keeping it flexed. Keep the thigh still and the knee turned out (see Figure G.9). This exercise can be done to the front, side, or back. It can also be done with the supporting leg on half-toe or demi-pointe.

Jumping and Turning Steps

The following terms are used when executing steps and combinations of steps in varied patterns or alone using a variety of space and direction. This basic dance vocabulary can be used to build a dance. However, there are many more words in the dance vocabulary. The terms and the execution of the steps mentioned here would be exacting if done in a formal dance class, but in this instance a reasonable facsimile gives the desired effect.

Figure G.8 Kick.

Figure G.9 Strike.

Steps which leave the floor are divided into three main categories:

- **Jumps**—When you leave the floor from two feet and land in basically the same position
- **Hops**—When the action starts and finishes all on the same foot
- **Leaps**—When the weight is transferred from one foot to another

big leap or **grand jeté** [grahn zhuh-TAY]—A leap through the air with the legs in a stretched position. The front or back leg can be bent in a stag position for variation.

foot exchange or **changement** [shahnzh-MAHN]—Start with feet in ballet fifth position. After a half-knee bend (demi-plié) jump off the floor and exchange feet so that you land with the other foot in front. Toes should be pointed while you are in the air and knees should be straight. You should land in a half-knee bend (demi-plié).

full, half, or **quarter turn jump** or **tour en l'air** [toor ahn LEHR]—This move is a combination jump step and turn step. It can be accomplished by starting with both feet on the floor and knees bent (demi-plié). Jump, lifting both feet off the floor and rotating in a single direction.

gallop or **chassé** [shah-SAY]—A sliding step that feels like a gallop but with pointed and turned-out feet.

glide or **glissade** [glee-SAHD]—This move starts in fifth position and in a half-knee bend (demi-plié). Brush (dégagé) the foot to second position lightly, then transfer the weight from the standing foot to the foot that has just lifted off the floor. Close the other foot to fifth position. This move can be done forward (en avant), side (à la seconde), or back (derriere). It is technically classified as a small leap.

hop or **temps levé** [tahn luh-VAY]—This move is a spring or hop on one foot with the raised leg in any position.

jump or **sauté** [soh-TAY]—Although the word means to jump it applies specifically to a jump that starts and finishes in the same position, such as first or second (see Figure G.10).

jumping jack or **échappé sauté** [ay-shah-PAY soh-TAY]—Starting in fifth or first position, jump to second position, landing in a half-knee bend (demi-plié) and springing back up and closing to fifth or first position (see Figure G.11).

leg beats in the air, bell click, or **cabriole** [kah-bree-AWL]—While standing on one foot, brush (dégagé) the other in any direction. Lift up off the floor in a hop or temps levé; at the top of the jump, beat or click legs together; open them as you come down, and land on one foot in a half-knee bend (demi-plié). Legs can be bent or straight

Figure G.10   Jump.   **Figure G.11**   Jumping jack.

in the air. When legs are bent, click your heels. When legs are straight in the air, beat your calves or thighs.

one-footed turn, **whirl**, or **pirouette** [peer-WHET]

- **Outside** or **en dehors**—Prepare by pointing (tendu) the right foot to the side, and place foot in back in fourth position with weight evenly distributed. Right arm is in front and left arm is to the side. At the same time open the right arm, raise the right leg, bent at the knee and touching the supporting leg with the toe (piqué position), rise up (relevé) on the left leg and make a revolution to the right. Plan to end in fifth position (see Figure G.12).

- **Inside** or **en dedans**—Prepare by pointing (tendu) the right foot to the side, and place foot in back in fourth position with weight evenly distributed. Left arm is in front and right arm to the side. At the same time open the left arm, raise the right leg, bent at the knee and touching the supporting leg with the toe (piqué position), rise up (relevé) on the left leg and make a revolution to the left. Plan to end in fifth position.

pivot on one foot or **promenade** [prah-muh-NAHD]—Stand on one foot with the other leg lifted off the floor. Make a circular move by pivoting the heel of the standing foot, rotating in the same direction until the desired number of revolutions are completed.

prance or **emboité** [ahn-bwah-TAY]—This move shifts weight from one leg to another. Start with one foot off the floor and the standing leg bent. Spring up and land on the raised foot (bent knee) with the other foot now lifted off the floor in the desired position.

run and leap or **pas de couru** [pah duh koo-REW], **grande jeté**— Take three running steps and a giant leap (see Figure G.13).

scissors jump or **sissonne** [see-SAWN]—Start with both feet on the floor in a half-knee bend (demi-plié). Jump off with both feet, pushing weight to one leg and landing on that one leg in a half-knee bend (demi-plié) (see Figure G.14).

seat turn or **sit spin**—This turn is accomplished by sitting on the floor, rotating on the buttocks with feet in desired position. Turn can be propelled gradually by pushing slowly with hands or by a big push to start.

three-step turn or **chainée** [sheh-NAY]—This turn is a chain going from second position facing forward to second position facing backwards. As you begin, the arms are open to second position when you face forward and closed to middle fifth when you face backwards. You keep rotating in the same direction, not back and forth like a washing machine.

turning steps—The body makes circular moves around an axis.

wrap turn or **soutenu** [soot-NEW]—This turn is accomplished by wrapping one foot around the other, tightly, and rotating your body in the direction of the standing foot, slowly unwrapping your feet and ending in fifth position (see Figure G.15).

Figure G.12 One-footed turn. **Figure G.13** Run and leap.

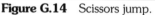

Figure G.14   Scissors jump.

Figure G.15   Wrap turn.

Linking Steps

The next series of steps can be termed "linking" steps because they can be used to join other steps and movements.

little steps or **bourrée** [boo-RAY]—Feet closed in a tight fifth position. Take tiny steps in any direction (working to keep the feet almost together). This step can also be done as a turn in place.

pas de basque [pah duh BAHSK]—Start in first position. Step to second position with right foot. Bring left foot in front to fourth position. Slide right foot to left foot into fifth position. This step can be reversed or done going backwards. It is often used in European folk dancing and can also be done with a leap from the first step to the second.

pas de bourrée [pah duh boo-RAY]—Start with right foot raised behind left ankle (coupé position). Step back behind you to fourth position, and with left foot step to second position. With right foot step forward to fourth position and lift the back leg to touch the ankle of the front leg (coupé position). You may also close to fifth position on the final step (see Figure G.16).

thank you or **révérence** [ray-vay-RAHNS]—A bow, usually at the end of class to thank the teacher, done in any fashion.

waltz, triplet—Move weight onto one foot with knee bent into a demi-plié. Reach out with the other foot onto half-toe or ball of the foot (demi-pointe). Do the same with the first foot. This completes one waltz, which is then continued in any direction or turning.

Directional and Descriptive Terms

These words may be used to describe how a dance movement should be performed.

à la seconde [ah lah suh-COHND]—to the side.

bound movement—Very controlled movement.

contra dancing—Dances where two lines are facing.

coupé [koo-PAY] **position**—With working foot touching front or back of supporting ankle.

demi-pointe—"Half toe," on the ball of the foot.

derriere [deh-reeYEHR]—To the back.

devant [duh-VAHN]—To the front.

en avant [ah nah-VAHN]—Forward.

en dedans [ahn duh-DAHN]—To the inside.

en dehors [ahn duh-AWR]—To the outside.

free movement—Open, spontaneous movement.

piqué [pee-KAY] **position**—The working leg is bent at the knee, with toe touching the supporting leg.

sur le coup de-pied [sewr luh KOO duh peeYAY]—Literally, "on the instep." The heel of the working leg is placed above the ankle of the supporting leg.

tendu [tahn-DEW]—Literally, "stretched." With leg extended or pointed.

a   b   c   d   e

Figure G.16 Pas de bourrée.

About the Authors

Susan McGreevy-Nichols has been teaching at Roger Williams Middle School in Providence, Rhode Island, since 1974. She is the founder and director of the inner-city school's nationally recognized dance program in which more than 300 of the school's 900 students elect to participate. Susan also lectures nationally on setting up dance programs in public schools, teaching dance as a nondancer, dance assessment, and writing grants for dance programs.

She has served as the president of the Rhode Island Association for Health, Physical Education, Recreation and Dance (RIAHPERD) and Vice President of Dance for the Eastern District of AAHPERD. She is on the National Dance Association's (NDA) Education Committee and is chair of the Rhode Island Alliance for Arts in Education.

In 1994 McGreevy-Nichols was named Rhode Island's Dance Teacher of the Year and in 1995 she was honored as the NDA National Dance Teacher of the Year. Susan lives in Coventry, Rhode Island, and enjoys travel, reading, and shopping.

Helene Scheff is director of ballet at Kingstown Dance Center, North Kingstown, Rhode Island; ballet consultant at Roger Williams Middle School in Providence, Rhode Island; and resident choreographer of the South County Players' Children's Theatre. She is also the administrative director of Chance to Dance, a statewide dance program that brings dance to children in grades 4 through 8.

Scheff has trained in New York, Chicago, and California. She is a former Joffrey Ballet dancer and has taught and choreographed for the University of

Kansas, University of Massachusetts at Amherst, and Rhode Island College.

She is Vice President of Dance for the Rhode Island AHPERD, serves on the Advocacy and Promotions committees for the NDA, and is treasurer for the Rhode Island Alliance for Arts in Education. Scheff lectures around the country on dance, fundraising, and dance administration. She is a founding member and past president of Dance Alliance of Rhode Island.

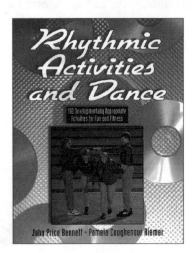